EAT WELL, WASTE LESS

An A–Z guide to using up leftovers

EAT WELL, WASTE LESS
An A–Z guide to using up leftovers

Bish Muir

green books

First published in 2008 by
Green Books
Foxhole, Dartington
Totnes, Devon TQ9 6EB
www.greenbooks.co.uk

Reprinted 2008, 2009, 2010, 2011

Printed in the UK by Latimer Trend, Plympton, Devon.
The text paper is made from 100% recycled post-consumer
waste, and the covers from 75% recycled material.

DISCLAIMER: The advice in this book is believed to be correct
at the time of printing, but the authors and publishers accept
no liability for actions inspired by this book.

ISBN 978 1 900322 37 9

Contents

Introduction

In the UK we throw away a third of the food we buy – 6.7 million tonnes every year

Nobody likes throwing away good food – quite apart from anything else, it is a terrible waste of money, as well as very harmful to the environment. However, with a little bit of guidance and inspiration we can all cut back on the amount of food waste we produce, and work towards having a guilt-free kitchen!

Cooking from leftovers came naturally to those who lived during the time of post-war rationing. They developed incredible powers of resourcefulness when it came to cooking, and would baulk at the idea of wasting 'good food' when it was hard to come by.

Further back in history we find an even more resourceful bunch than our grandmothers and great grandmothers: the 'bijoutiers' who emerged in Paris and Versailles in the eighteenth and nineteenth centuries. They would go around to the grand houses, hotels and restaurants in the city, and collect the leftover food in big baskets. Much of the food would have been totally untouched and, once collected, the food could be rearranged on little plates and sold at the markets and even back into restaurants! The name 'bijoutiers' comes from the fact that the food was arranged on the plate to look like 'bijoux' – 'little jewels'.

Unfortunately these resourceful skills have not always been passed down through the generations and we now live in a largely 'throw away' society. Excessive food waste is an even greater problem now than it was back in the eighteenth and nineteenth centuries because it is no longer restricted to the privileged classes.

Today food is more plentiful, but there is no reason why using our leftovers should be considered a dying skill. Cooking ingredients have never been so accessible to us, and with a stock of simple ingredients in the cupboard, great results can be achieved.

The unpalatable facts

- Of the 6.7 million tonnes of food that are thrown away every year in the UK, 4.1 million tonnes is unopened and untouched. Of this, 340,000 tonnes is still 'in date'. This is largely a result of a lack of meal planning, but also of over-supply – 1.2 million tonnes of food waste is simply left on our plates!

- The average household throws away between £15,000 and £24,000 worth of food in a lifetime – up to £610 per household per year

- In a recent survey, 68% of people who admitted to throwing away food cared about it, because they viewed it as a waste of money as well as a waste of good food.

- Food waste is increasing at a rate of 15% every decade.

- Every year we throw away 5.1 million whole potatoes, 2.8 million whole tomatoes, 1 million slices of ham and 1.2 million sausages. Rather than throwing them away, these should be considered 'gems' as they can provide the basis for so many delicious meals, for example soups, stir fries and omelettes.

We can do something about it!

Whether you have a household of fussy eaters or live on your own, this book will help you reduce the amount of food you throw away, and save money at the same time.

Why should we reduce our food waste?

Rotting food buried in landfill sites generates methane, a greenhouse gas over twenty times more potent than carbon dioxide and a major contributor to climate change. So serious is the problem, in fact, that it is estimated that if we stopped throwing away food that could be eaten, we could make carbon savings equivalent to taking one in five cars off the road!

In addition to producing methane, rotting food in landfill sites also produces leachate, a liquid produced when water (from rain) passes through the waste. The leachates collect at the base of the landfill and are a potentially hazardous waste, causing pollution to groundwater and the environment, which can cause health problems.

As well as the above, it is an uncomfortable fact that while we waste millions of tonnes of perfectly edible food, people are still dying of hunger in the third world.

Whether our incentive is to save the environment or the money in our wallets, the government has made a commitment to reduce food waste in landfill to 35% of 1995 levels by 2020, which means we all have to do our bit. Reducing food waste is one of a number of really practical ways in which we can help slow down climate change, and if it reduces our shopping bills and produces tasty results then we're all quids in!

Essential tools of the trade

You don't need a kitchen that is stuffed full of electrical gadgets and trendy gismos to produce fabulous meals, but there are a few 'must-have' items which will give you the equipment you need to make the most of the recipes in this book.

- *Bottle opener* – the great accompaniment for every good cook!

- *Can opener* – one that fixes to the wall is the best option.

- *Cheese grater* – try and get one that comes with a sealable container so that you can store any leftover grated cheese.

- *Heavy casserole dish* – ideal for cooking soups and stews on the top of the stove and finishing off slowly in the oven.

- *Food processor* – so useful for making soups and smoothies.

- *Microwave* – not essential but, for ease and speed, very handy for re-heating leftovers.

- *Plastic clips* – these prevent spillage and keeps things fresh for longer. *Clothes pegs or elastic bands* do the same job.

- *Pyrex dish* – very useful when microwaving food, or re-heating in the oven.

- *Selection of airtight containers* – empty ice cream containers will do, but there is nothing to beat those with a special rubber seal. This keeps leftovers really fresh and avoids contamination and nasty smells in your fridge.

- *Sharp knife* – essential for preparing food easily.

- *Weighing scales* – essential for getting the correct amounts of ingredients.

- *Wooden knife block* or *knife magnet* – a good way to store your knives as it protects the blades and makes them easy to find!

- *Wooden spoons* – for using with a non-stick pan.

- *Wok or large non-stick frying pan* – stir fries and quick curries are a good way to use up a single carrot, onion, etc.

It is essential to keep all kitchen equipment really clean and stored in a place that is both easy to get at and safe from dirt and children.

'Must-have' ingredients in the cupboard and fridge

There are a number of ingredients which come up time and again in cooking, and they form the backbone of your recipes. They are there to provide flavour and substance, and as long as you keep these vital ingredients stocked up at all times, you will be able to create something – however basic.

Much of the list below will store well, so you can afford to buy a reasonable quantity without fear of it going off or getting stale, provided it is stored correctly. This is a perfect example of where storage containers and clips can be so useful for storing opened food and half-empty packets.

- *Baked beans* – a very good source of protein and great for an instant meal.

- *Canned tomatoes* –these are one of the basic ingredients for pasta sauces and soups and will obviously store for months.

- *Canned pulses* – chickpeas and lentils add substance to soups and stews.

- *Cans of tuna* – fabulous with a baked potato and mayonnaise, for spicing up a salad or adding to a pasta sauce.

- *Cheese* – a good hunk of mature cheddar adds taste and substance to many dishes. Keep the cheese wrapped up in cling film or greaseproof paper to avoid it drying out. If you get a bit of mould on the edges, just cut it off – it won't affect the rest of the cheese.

- *Eggs* – whether it's Spanish omelettes, simple cakes or just scrambled egg on toast, it's always good to have half a dozen eggs in the house. Free range eggs definitely taste better and have beautiful deep orange yolks that add colour to your cooking.

- *Flour* – essential for sauces, e.g. cheese sauce for macaroni cheese, and for baking.

- *Herbs and spices* – as well as a few fresh herbs if you have room, the following dried herbs are very useful: basil, oregano, rosemary, tarragon, mint, parsley, thyme, marjoram and mixed herbs. Useful spices include ground ginger, ground coriander, chilli powder and curry powder.

- *Mayonnaise* – always keep a jar in the fridge. It lasts for ages and goes with chicken, potatoes, tuna and just about anything that fits inside a sandwich!

- *Rice or pasta* – rice or pasta dishes, using leftover meat, vegetables and cheese, are easy to rustle up, and both of these staples store very well.

- *Oils* – whilst a good vegetable or sunflower oil is essential for frying food, olive oil, although more expensive, is delicious for salad dressings. Sesame oil is fantastic for stir fries as it has a rich, nutty taste.

- *Onions and garlic* – store these in a dry, cool place and they will last for several weeks. These are essential for any casserole or sauce, and will add taste to just about anything.

- *Ready-made sauces* – always good to have in the cupboard for adding to leftover meat or vegetables.

- *Seasoning* – *sugar, salt, pepper* and mustard.

- *Soy sauce* – great for adding to stir fries.

- *Stock cubes* – you can make your own stock from meat or chicken carcasses (see pp.76-7), but stock cubes are quick and easy to use, and are great for making simple soups. Vegetable stock cubes help to add real flavour in a leftover vegetable soup, or when used in a risotto instead of water.

- *Worcestershire sauce* – delicious with beef dishes such as cottage pie and bolognaise.

If it helps, keep a list of these items on the wall or by the door so that when you run out you can make a note to replace them next time you go shopping.

Planning your shopping

- A third of us go shopping without a list.

- In a recent survey 22% of people who were asked why they threw away so much food, said that it was because they bought too much.

- Another 22% claimed they were tempted by multi-packs but then did not plan their week's meals, so that the extra food remained unused and had to be thrown away.

- 34% admitted to throwing away food because it had gone past the 'use by' or 'best before' date.

- Research shows that people who plan their weekly shop are less likely to over-purchase and so less inclined to throw away unwanted or unused food.

Keep an eye on 'use-by' dates

It is a good idea to plan your weekly menus by the 'use by' dates on the food you buy. Obviously, something with a shorter shelf life should be used early on, with any leftovers being used to create a stir fry or soup for later in the week.

Make the most of what you buy

Here is an example of good planning which gets the most out of your food and makes your money go further: buy a whole chicken together with some vegetables, cook it to have a roast on one day and then strip the carcass to use the remaining meat for a risotto or other chicken dish in a couple of days time, and use the bones for stock.

Menu planning example:

Sunday: Large roast chicken, roast potatoes, carrots and peas. Strip chicken carcass and make stock (p.77) from the bones and any leftover vegetables.

Monday: Chicken sandwiches for school/work packed lunch, and risotto (p.59) for evening meal using leftover peas and some mushrooms with plenty of parmesan.

Tuesday: Use up leftover roast potatoes by slicing and frying them. Serve with sausages and vegetables.

Wednesday: Chicken Crunch (p.90), using rest of cold chicken.

Thursday: Chicken soup (p.72) made with stock made on Sunday. The soup will freeze well for another occasion.

Buy in season

If you can, buy local food that is in season. Not only is it much fresher and tastier (having not been chilled and shipped or flown half way around the world to get to the supermarket shelves), but it is generally cheaper.

Avoid 'BOGOFs' which don't store easily

BOGOF (Buy One Get One Free) offers are fine if it is something like mince that can go straight into the freezer, but with perishable food that won't freeze it isn't good value if the 'free' item goes mouldy before you get around to eating it. Be realistic about what you can eat in a week (or next few days) before you buy – good planning saves you having to throw away food that you simply have not managed to get around to eating.

Don't shop when you're hungry

The best way to avoid buying too much food is to make sure you avoid shopping when you're feeling really hungry, as any planning may go completely out of the window! Shopping without children, if at all possible, is also a good idea as it helps you to concentrate and plan.

Storing leftovers

Care must be taken when storing leftovers – here are a few basic rules:

- Always let cooked food cool down fully before it is put in the fridge.

- Don't leave food out overnight, as this can cut its shelf life significantly.

- Different foods should be prepared and stored separately. To prevent the spread of bacteria, raw meat should be stored on the bottom shelf of the fridge (or in a tightly sealed container) so that it doesn't drip on to cooked other food. Meat and dairy should be stored on separate shelves wherever possible.

- Keep your fridge at the right temperature: between 1° and 5°C is the optimum. It's a good idea to buy a magnetic fridge thermometer for the inside of your fridge.

- If you cook more than you need, freeze what is left over in an airtight container for another time.

- Few people have the luxury of a cool larder or dairy, so there can be occasions when the fridge gets rather over-full. This can be avoided with careful planning: make sure you don't take up valuable fridge space with things that don't necessarily need to be in a cool environment.

- Many packaged or tinned foods carry storage instructions, so it's a good idea to read these carefully.

Storage times for common leftovers

FOOD	HOW TO STORE	MAX. STORAGE TIME	SUITABLE FOR FREEZING?
Cooked meat	Preferably leave on the bone to avoid drying out. Cover with foil. Alternatively strip meat from the bone and wrap well in foil. Store in fridge.	2-3 days	YES
Cooked chicken or turkey	As above. Store in fridge.	2-3 days	YES
Cooked fish	Cover with foil. Store in fridge.	1-2 days	YES
Cooked vegetables	Plastic container or cover with clingfilm. Store in fridge.	3-5 days	NO
Cooked stews and casseroles	Cover well with foil or store in dish with lid. Store in fridge.	2-4 days	YES
Milk puddings or custard	Cover with clingfilm. Store in fridge.	2-3 days	NO
Raw fruit salad	Cover with clingfilm. Store in fridge.	3-4 days	NO
Grated cheese	Sealed container. Store in fridge.	10-14 days	YES
Egg whites	Container with lid. Store in fridge.	4-5 days	
Egg yolks	Cover with water and store in covered container with clingfilm. Store in fridge.	3-4 days	NO
Breadcrumbs	Sealed plastic bag. Store in fridge.	3 weeks	YES

Re-heating food safely

It is essential to re-heat leftover food quickly and thoroughly. Re-heated food should not be kept at a 'tepid' temperature for any length of time as this can encourage bacteria to develop. The core temperature must be at least 82°C – if in doubt, use a food thermometer.

Ideally, food should be taken straight from the fridge or cool larder to a hot oven, hob or microwave for re-heating; remember that leftover food should only be re-heated once.

If you are using an oven or hob, make sure you stir the food occasionally so that it heats right through and is piping hot.

Rice

It is safe to re-heat rice so long as the rice has been refrigerated quickly after being cooked the first time, and is no more than a day old. Dangerous bacteria only develop in cooked rice if it is left at room temperature for any length of time. Rice should be re-heated quickly and thoroughly to prevent any possibility of bacteria developing.

Meat

Slice, mince or cube meat before re-heating to ensure it heats through evenly.

Re-heating using a microwave

- Always consult your microwave manual for cooking and re-heating times.

- Cover foods with a lid (vented) or a microwave-safe plastic wrap to hold in moisture and provide safe, even heating. Moisture is important for microwave cooking, so it may be advisable to add a couple of spoonfuls of water to the food if it is rather dry.

- It is important when re-heating that food is given the recommended amount of time (consult your microwave manual). As with conventional ovens, food should be piping hot when removed from the microwave and allowed to cool as necessary.

- Stir the food occasionally to avoid 'cold spots' and ensure that all parts of the food are thoroughly heated through.

- Food continues to cook for a short time after you have removed it from the microwave, so allow it to stand for 1-2 minutes before serving in order to ensure that the cooking process is complete. (This known as 'Standing Time'.)

- To be really safe, use a food thermometer to check that your food has reached a safe internal temperature – leftover food should be re-heated to at least 82°C.

'Use by' dates and other instructions

What the terms mean:

'Use by'

This means exactly that. Officially, food and drink should not be consumed after the end of the 'use by' date shown on the label. With meat and fish this is definitely the case, even if it may smell and look fine. Although officially dairy should also not be used after the 'use by' date, slightly off milk is perfect for making scones and will not make you ill; and within reason, cheese can still be eaten even when there is a little mould on it, provided you remove the mould.

Remember that 'use by' dates are only applicable if the storage instructions on the label are adhered to, as otherwise food might go off before its 'use by' date.

'Sell by' or 'Display until'

These are instructions for shop staff to tell them when they should take a product off the shelves, and do not mean that the food cannot be eaten after that date. In fact, one manufacturer of yoghurts, Stonyfield Farm, actually states on its website "It can be perfectly okay to eat yoghurt after the sell-by date. Just use your judgment. If the yoghurt looks, smells, and tastes good, and there are no visible signs of mould, it's okay to eat."

'Best before'

Eggs should not be eaten after the 'best before' date, or if the shells are cracked

'Best before' is usually applied to foods that last longer, such as tinned food or frozen or dried food such as pasta. It should be safe to eat food after the 'best before' date, but the food will no longer be at its best and may begin to lose its flavour and texture. The best thing to do is to plan your menus around the dates on the food, so that if you know that something is coming up to the end of its life you can make sure you eat it on or before that day.

Composting

Up to a third of our household waste can be composted

Composting your fruit and vegetable peelings, apple cores, tea bags, egg shells etc., rather than putting them in the bin, reduces the amount of rotting food in landfill sites. You don't need a big garden to do this. There are some fantastic wormeries and mini compost systems on the market that will sit comfortably on a patio or balcony, and children love wormeries – there is something fascinating about watching the worms at work!

Most council websites will tell you how to get hold of compost bins and wormeries, and many will be able to offer them at much reduced prices. In addition, many councils have set up local community-based composting schemes where people can take their food waste and other compostables to a communal site and, in return, buy the resulting compost back to put on their gardens.

There are many benefits of composting. Not only do you reduce your waste but you are producing fantastic nutrient-rich compost for your gardens or pot plants.

You can easily compost:

- Fruit and vegetables and their peelings
- Tea bags and leaves, coffee grounds
- Cardboard, e.g. cut up cereal packets and egg boxes
- Egg shells (crushed)

You need a sealed composting system to compost:

- Meat
- Fish
- Cooked food

You can't compost these safely:

- Cat litter
- Dog faeces

For more detailed information, get a book such as *Composting: an easy household guide* by Nicky Scott.

Packaging

It's generally best to buy food loose where possible rather than pre-packaged, because if you buy pre-packaged, you can't choose an exact amount and will often end up buying more than you need. Also, pre-packaged food will always cost more, as the cost of the packaging is passed on to the customer. It is always a good idea to buy your perishable food loose, especially if you are only buying for one or two people. That way you are only buying what you think you need and are less likely to waste any – and you will save money. You will also reduce the amount of waste going to landfill.

However, there are ways in which you can make use of the packaging from supermarkets, for example:

- Reuse plastic containers from tomatoes etc. for seed trays – perfect for growing herbs or cress.

- Reuse yoghurt pots for children's paint pots or for storing elastic bands etc.

- Reuse soup pots for freezing stock, or your home-made soup.

- Reuse ice cream containers for storing food or small toys.

- Collect your plastic containers or bottles, and give them to your local primary school for their art and craft lessons.

Food miles

Some grapes on our supermarket shelves have travelled over 7,000 miles from Chile, whilst apples from New Zealand may have travelled a staggering 10,000 miles.

By food miles, we mean the distance our food travels from its original growing place to our plates, including journeys made to be produced, processed, packaged and displayed in the shop. Large amounts of fuel are used to move the food from one place to the next, whether by air, sea or road, all of which has a huge impact on the environment.

We have already looked at the benefits to your wallet of buying food in season wherever possible, but if we want to protect the environment, it is important to consider how far food has travelled to get to our shops, and buy locally grown food in season whenever possible.

How to use this book

Leftovers can be divided into two types:

- **The cooked food that has been left after a meal or is simply unused due to bad planning.**

- **The leftover which takes the form of the single carrot, leek, parsnip, tomato, sausage, slice of ham or egg in the fridge or cupboard. These often get discarded because on their own they do not constitute a big enough portion to provide a meal for the household.**

The book is divided into three sections:

The A-Z

This features both types of leftover (see above) and gives you quick and easy recipes, cross references to the main recipes, and other ideas for using up and storing the leftover.

Basic Recipes

These are recipes which can be adapted according to the leftover, e.g. 'Basic Stock' or 'Basic Stir Fry'.

Individual Recipes

These are recipes which work best with specific leftover ingredients e.g. 'Bubble and Squeak', and 'Fish Cakes'.

Key to symbols

(L)	Uncooked leftover – single item, or not enough to make a meal/last drops in the pot
(C)	Cooked leftover
(S)	Ingredients from the store cupboard
(O)	Over-ripe or old
(B)	Basic recipe

⏱ Time to prepare (in minutes)   ⏱ Time to cook (in minutes)

A-Z of leftover ingredients

with quick and easy recipes and tips

A-Z of leftover ingredients

Unless specified, all recipes are for four servings.

APPLES *(O)*
Recipes Basic: crumble (p.50), fruit salad (p.53), smoothies (p.69), stewed fruit (p.73).
Individual: Apple and Cinnamon Fritters (p.82), Fruit Juices (p.94).
Quick and easy cook cored, peeled and chopped apple in a little water, a pinch of cinnamon
and some lemon zest for about 10 minutes to make apple sauce. Delicious with pork.
Tip Cheapest to buy in late summer and early winter.
See also Pears.

APRICOTS *(C/L)*
Recipes Basic: crumble (p.50), fruit salad (p.53), stewed fruit (p.73).
Quick and easy Chop cooked, raw or dried apricots into little pieces and sprinkle on your ce-
real. Add raw or cooked apricots to a pork casserole or serve with pork chops.

AVOCADO *(L)*
Recipes Basic: salad (p.62).
Quick and easy Slice up and serve with sliced tomato and vinaigrette.
Tip To ripen avocados, put in a warm spot in a paper bag with a banana. Sprinkling with
lemon/lime juice will prevent cut avocado discolouring.

BACON *(C/L)*
Recipes Basic: pie (p.55), quiche (p.58), risotto (p.59), salad (p.62), sauce (p.65). Individual:
Baked Potato Fillings (p.84), Bubble and Squeak (p.89), Macaroni Cheese (p.99), Spanish
Omelette (p.103), Stuffed Peppers (p.104).
Quick and easy Bacon sandwich with lettuce, tomatoes and mayonnaise.
Tip Chop up cooked bacon and sprinkle on salads, baked potatoes, pizzas.

BAKED BEANS (CANNED) *(S)*

Recipes Individual: Baked Potato Fillings (p.84)

Tip Add any leftover Baked Beans to casseroles.

Quick and easy Baked beans on toast with grated cheese on top or a slice of ham or even a fried egg.

Can also be used in shepherd's/cottage pie (p.56).

BAKED POTATO *(C)*

Recipes Individual: Baked Cheesy Potatoes (p.83), Baked Potato Fillings (p.84).

Quick and easy Slice up leftover baked potatoes and fry in hot oil to make 'chips'.

See also Beef.

BANANAS *(O)*

Recipes Basic: fruit salad (p.53), smoothie (p.69). Individual: Banana and Chocolate Digestive Pudding (p.86).

Quick and easy Slice a banana longways and fill with pieces of chocolate. Wrap banana in foil and bake for about 15 minutes.

Tip Bananas emit a gas that ripens fruit so keep bananas separate from the rest of the fruit bowl. Bananas that are a bit brown are still great for smoothies or some puddings

Can also be used in Apple and Cinnamon Fritters (p.82).

See also Pancakes, Yoghurt.

BEANS (CANNED) *(S)*

Recipes Basic: salad (p.62), soup (p.72). Individual: Bean and Onion Stew (p.87), Chilli con carne (p.91).

Tip It is always useful to keep canned beans (e.g. borlotti, cannellini, butter) in your store cupboard as they can be used to bulk out soup or stew, or make the basis of a salad.

BEANS (FRESH) *(C/L)*
See 'Baked beans', Broad beans', French beans', 'runner beans'.

BEEF *(C)*
Recipes Basic: curry (p.52), pie (p.55-6), rissoles (p.60), salad (p.62), stir fry (p.74), stock (p.76).
Individual: Chilli con Carne (p.91), Lamb Pitta Pockets (p.97).
Quick and Easy Serve cold roast beef sliced with a baked potato and horseradish sauce.
Tips Cooked beef can be minced in a food processor or mincer.

BEER *(O)*
Recipes Basic: pie (p.55), sauce (p.64).
Tip Keep any flat beer – it's a great addition to stews and pies, adding flavour to the sauce.

BISCUITS *(O)*
Recipes Basic: crumble (p.50). Individual: Banana and Chocolate Digestive Pudding (p.86)
Tip Crumbs or old biscuits from the bottom of the biscuit tin can be used as toppings for many puddings, or as the base for a cheesecake.

BLACKBERRIES/BLUEBERRIES *(L/O)*
Recipes Basic: crumble (p.50), fruit salad (p.53), smoothies (p.69) and stewed fruit (p.73).
Individual: Fruit Juices (p.94), Summer Pudding (p.105).
Tip Blackberries can be picked from the hedgerows in early autumn. They can be frozen on a tray in the freezer and stored in freezer bags.

BLACKCURRANTS *(L/O)*
Recipes Basics: crumble (p.50), fruit salad (p.53), smoothies (p.69) and stewed fruit (p.73).
Individual: Fruit Juices (p.94), Summer Pudding (p.105).
Tip Freeze as for Blackberries.

BLUEBERRIES *(L/O)*

Recipes Basic: crumble (p.50), fruit salad (p.53), smoothies (p.69) and stewed fruit (p.73). Individual: Fruit Juices (p.94), Summer Pudding (p.105).
Quick and easy Add to cereal or yoghurt

BOLOGNAISE *(C)*

Quick and easy Heat up and serve with a thick slice of bread and butter.
Can also be used in Baked Potato Fillings (p.84).

BREAD *(S)*

Recipes Individual: Bread and Butter Pudding (p.88), Summer Pudding (p.105).
Quick and easy For bread sauce (delicious with roast chicken or turkey), heat some milk in a saucepan with cloves, half an onion and bay leaf simmer for 30 mins, remove onion cloves and bay leaf, add bread crumbs until sauce is required thickness.
Tips Make breadcrumbs by processing old bread in a food processor until all lumps are removed. Freeze in freezer bags and use when needed. Make croutons, to put in salads and soup, by frying cubed old bread in oil until brown, or coating in olive oil and baking in the oven until brown. If bread rolls or pitta seem a little stale, wet the outside with water and stick in a hot oven for about 2 minutes, this will refresh the bread nicely. Put pieces of greaseproof paper between slices of bread before freezing – then only use the number of slices you need.
Can also be used in Chicken Crunch (p.90), Fish Cakes (p.93).

BROAD BEANS *(C/L)*
Recipes Basic: crumble (p.51), curry (p.52), salad (p.62), stir fry (p.74). Individual: Vegetable Stew (p.106).
Quick and easy Add cold broad beans to a salad; try coating in mayonnaise and black pepper.

BROCCOLI *(C/L)*
Recipes Basic: crumble (p.51), curry (p.52), pie (p.57), quiche (p.58), risotto (p.59), sauce (pp.65-6), soup (p.72), stir fry (p.74). Individual: Bubble and Squeak (p.89). Chicken Crunch (p.90).
Tip Avoid overcooking – it is best steamed.

BRUSSELS SPROUTS *(C)*
Recipes Basic: pie (p.57), soup (p.72). Individual: Bubble and Squeak (p.89).
Quick and easy Cold Brussels sprouts can be tossed in a saucepan with hot butter, almonds and black pepper and heated through, or served cold with some cold turkey and cranberry sauce.
Tip Cheapest in early winter when in season.

BURGERS *(C)*
Recipes Basic: pie (p.55), tomato sauce (p.65).
Quick and easy Crumble up cold leftover burgers and add them to a pasta sauce or shepherd's pie.

CABBAGE (GREEN) *(C/L)*
Recipes Basic: crumble (p.51), soup (p.72), stir fry (p.74). Individual: Bubble and Squeak (p.89).
Quick and easy Toss leftover cabbage in butter, black pepper and mustard seed until heated through.

CABBAGE (RED) *(C/L)*

Recipe Individual: Bubble and squeak (p.89).

Quick and easy Cooked red cabbage can be heated up again. Toss it in some melted butter and try adding a pinch of nutmeg and some raisins or sultanas. Raw red cabbage can be shredded or finely sliced and added to a coleslaw or salad.

CARROTS *(C/L)*

Recipes Basic: crumble (p.51), curry (p.52), pie (p.57), roast vegetables (p.61), salad (p.62), sauce (p.64), soup (p.72) , stir fry (p.74), stock (pp.76-8). Individual: Vegetable Stew (p.106).

Quick and easy Use grated carrots in a green salad or to make carrot salad with raisins and lemon vinaigrette (p.66).

Tip Use up raw carrots by slicing them lengthways and using them with dips, or houmous for a tasty and nutritious snack.

CAULIFLOWER *(C/L)*

Recipe Basic: crumble (p.51), sauce (p.66), stir fry (p.74).

Quick and easy Any leftover raw cauliflower can be cut into florets and eaten with dips such as cream cheese dip, houmous or taramasalata. Cooked cauliflower can be added to a stir fry or curry.

Tip Up to 90% of the goodness of vegetables can be lost by boiling them in water. Wherever possible, steam your vegetables instead to retain the goodness.

CELERY *(L)*

Recipes Basic: curry (p.52), pie (p.57), salad (p.62), soup (p.72), stir fry (p.74), stock (p.78). Individual: Vegetable Stew (p.106).

Quick and easy Slice lengthways and use with a dip.

Tip Celery lasts much longer if it is kept in the fridge and you can eat the leaves as well.

CEREALS (BREAKFAST) *(S)*

Recipes Individual: Chocolate Crispy Cakes (p.92).

Tips Always fold down the top of the plastic inner packaging when storing cereals as they will keep fresh longer. Old cornflakes can usually be made crispy again by laying them out on a baking sheet and cooking them in a hot oven for about 3 minutes.

CHEESE *(L)*

Recipes Basic: quiche (p.58), salad (p.62), sauce (p.66). Individual: Baked Cheesy Potatoes (p.83) Chicken Crunch (p.90), Macaroni Cheese (p.99), Spanish Omelette (p.103). Welsh Rarebit (p.107).

Quick and easy Cheese on toast. Try spreading mustard on the toast before putting the cheese on. Also great with a slice of ham underneath the cheese.

Tips Store in an airtight container, cling film or greaseproof paper. If cheese gets a bit hard or mouldy at the edge, don't worry, just cut the mouldy bits it off and use the hard bits grated in a sauce, or on top of a shepherds pie.

See also Crisps, Ham, Pancakes, Potatoes, Spinach.

CHERRIES *(L)*

Recipes crumble (p.50), fruit salad (p.53). Individual: Fruit Juices (p.94).

Quick and easy If cherries are getting a little old, halve them, take out the stone and add them to yoghurt or on top of muesli.

CHICKEN *(C)*

Recipes Basic: curry (p.52), pie (p.54), risotto (p.59), rissoles (p.60), salad (p.62), soup (p.72), stir fry (p.74), stock (p.77).
Individual: Baked Potato Fillings (p.84), Chicken Crunch (p.90), Lamb Pitta Pockets (p.97). Macaroni Cheese (p.99).

Quick and easy Coronation chicken – mix the cold, cooked chicken with mayonnaise, a teaspoon of curry powder, a dessert spoon of tomato purée and some raisins. Delicious in the summer with new potatoes and also a great way to use up leftover turkey.

Tip When stripping the meat from a roast chicken carcass, it is much easier to do it when the meat is still warm. Make sure you have clean hands.

CHICKPEAS (CANNED) *(S)*

Recipes Basic: soup (p.72). Individual: Bean and Onion Stew (p.87).
Quick and easy Blend a tin of chickpeas with some garlic, olive oil, lemon juice and tahini (sesame paste) to make a delicious houmous dip.
Tip Tinned chickpeas are great for bulking out a soup or stew.

CHILLIES *(S)*

Recipes Basic: soup (p.72), stir fry (p.74). Individual: Chilli con Carne (p.91).
Quick and easy Marinade meat or chicken for at least an hour in chopped chillies with lime or lemon juice before cooking.
Tip After cutting chillies, make sure you wash your hands straight away and do not rub your eyes! Dried chillies can be used in casseroles and curries – they are a little hotter than fresh ones.

CHOCOLATE *(L)*

Recipe Individual: Chocolate Crispy Cakes (p.92).
Quick and easy Melt any leftover chocolate in a bowl over a saucepan of boiling water and pour over ice cream or grate it over sweet puddings to add a little cheer.
Tip Always store in an airtight container.
See also Bananas.

CHRISTMAS PUDDING *(C)*

Quick and easy Slice the Christmas pudding and fry in a little butter. Serve with cream or brandy butter.

COFFEE *(L)*

Recipe Individual: Iced Coffee (p.96).
Quick and easy Add a little strong cold coffee to a chocolate sauce to pour over ice cream or a chocolate sponge. (Not advisable for children).

COURGETTES (C/L)

Recipes crumble (p.51), pie (p.57), quiche (p.58), roast vegetables (p.61), sauce (p.65), stir fry (p.74). Individual: Vegetable Stew (p.106).
Quick and easy Slice and fry in some butter and garlic and serve with lots of black pepper.
Can also be used in Spanish Omelette (p.103).

COUSCOUS (C)

Recipe Basic: salad (p.62).
Quick and easy Leftover couscous can be used instead of rice, served with cold meats or roasted vegetables.

CREAM (L)

Recipes Basic: quiche (p.58), sauce (p.66), soup (p.72). Individual: Bread and Butter Pudding (p.88).
Quick and easy Add a dollop of cream to sauces, stews or casseroles to thicken.

CRÈME FRAÎCHE (L)

Recipes Basic: curry (p.52), sauce (p.66).
Individual: Baked Cheesy Potatoes (p.83), Baked Potato Fillings (p.84).
Quick and easy If you have a little bit of crème fraîche left in the pot, add a dollop on top of tomato-based pasta dishes or of fruit puddings.
See also Peaches.

CRISPS (S)

Recipes Basic: Vegetable crumble (p.51). Individual: Chicken Crunch (p.90).
Quick and easy Crunch up old crisps and scatter on top of fish pie with some grated cheese.

CRUMBLE (B)

Recipes Basic: Fruit and vegetable crumble (p.50 and p.51).
Quick and easy Add cream or custard to a re-heated fruit crumble to avoid it tasting too dry.
Tip If you make too much crumble topping, freeze it and use it another time.

CUCUMBER *(L)*

Recipes Basic: salad (p.62).

Quick and easy Chop up the cucumber finely and mix with natural yoghurt, chopped mint and a crushed clove of garlic to make tsatsiki. Delicious as a dip or to eat with pitta bread.

Tip If you have half a cucumber leftover, slice it up and put it in a jar of spiced vinegar and keep for two months; great with a ploughman's lunch.

See also Kidney Beans (canned), Rice.

CURRY *(B)*

Recipe Basic: curry (p.52). Individual: Baked Potato Fillings (p.84).

Quick and easy Don't throw away the remains of a takeaway curry. It can easily be heated up the next day; Meat-based curries should not be kept for more than 2 days in the fridge after purchase.

CUSTARD *(L)*

Recipes Basic: Fruit crumble (p.50), stewed fruit (p.73).

Quick and easy Custard is one of life's little treats, and can easily be re-heated if left over. Try warming it up and adding a chopped-up banana.

EGGS *(L)*

Recipes Basic: quiche (p.58), salad (p.62). Individual: Spanish Omelette (p.103).

Quick and easy For a quick omelette, whisk two eggs in a bowl, season with salt and pepper. Melt an teaspoon of butter in a non-stick frying pan, pour in the egg mixture and cook for about 7 minutes, until all the egg has hardened.

Tips Use eggs as soon as possible after purchase, and certainly before their 'use by' date. Don't use eggs with cracked shells. Use leftover scrambled egg to make an egg and mayonnaise sandwich.

Can also be used in white sauce (p.66).

See also Spinach.

FISH (C)

Recipes Basic: stock (p.75). Individual: Fish Cakes (p.93).

Quick and easy Oily fish such as pilchards, sardines and anchovies can be added to a salad, or the top of a pizza or mushed up on toast.

Tip Fish will only stay fresh in the fridge for about 3-4 days so good menu planning is needed.

FRENCH BEANS (C/L)

Recipes Basic: curry (p.52), pie (p.57), risotto (p.59), salad (p.62), stir fry (p.74). Individual: Vegetable Stew (p.106).

Quick and easy Cold French beans are delicious just tossed in a little vinaigrette and lots of black pepper.

Can also be used in Spanish Omelette (p.103).

See also Potatoes.

FROMAGE FRAIS (L)

Recipes fruit salad (p.53), quiche (p.58), salad (p.62), sauce (p.66).

Quick and easy If you have a little bit left in the bottom of the pot, this is delicious as a substitute for cream on puddings and fruit.

See also Ham, Peaches.

FRUIT (C/L)

Recipes Basic: crumble (p.50), stewed fruit (p.73).

See also individual fruits, e.g. Apple.

FRUIT SALAD (B)

Recipes Basic: fruit salad (p.53).

Tip Leftover fruit salad is delicious on top of cereal. Fruit salad is a good way of using up old or slightly bruised fruit. Almost any fruit can be used.

GAMMON (L)

See: 'Ham'.

GARLIC *(L)*

Recipes Basic: pie (p.55), roast vegetables (p.61), salad (p.62), sauce (p.65), soup (p.72).
Quick and easy Slice a loaf of French bread and butter the slices with a mixture of crushed garlic and butter. Put the loaf together again, wrap in aluminium foil and bake in the oven at 150°C/300°F/gas mark 2 for 10 minutes.
Can also be used in stews and numerous cooked dishes.
See also Cucumber.

GRAPEFRUIT *(L/O)*

Recipes Basic: fruit salad (p.53). Individual: Fruit Juices (p.94).
Tip If the grapefruit is a bit old, the zest can be used to add flavour to fruit puddings.
Quick and easy Cut grapefruit in half and sprinkle each half with soft brown or muscovado sugar. Pop under a hot grill for 5 minutes until the sugar melts.

GRAPES *(L/O)*

Recipes Basic: curry (p.52), fruit salad (p.53), risotto (p.59). Individual: Fruit Juices (p.94).
Tip Add to a curry or risotto at the last minute for extra flavour.
Quick and easy Chop into some natural or flavoured yoghurt and sprinkle some muesli or crunchy cereal on top for a quick pudding. A dollop of honey or maple syrup on top makes it even more delicious.

GRAVY *(L)*

Recipes Basic: Pie (pp.54-6).
Tip Leftover gravy is ideal for adding flavour to a savoury pie.
Quick and easy Re-heat gravy and pour it over cooked meat or vegetables.

GREENS *(C)*

Recipe Basic: Bubble and Squeak (p.89).
Quick and easy Cooked greens can be heated up by tossing them in hot melted butter and black pepper in a saucepan for a couple of minutes. Add chopped ham or chopped tomatoes.

HAM *(C/L)*

Recipes Basic: pie (p.55), quiche (p.58), risotto (p.59), salad (p.62), sauce (p.65-6). Individual: Macaroni Cheese (p.99), Spanish Omelette (p.103), Welsh Rarebit (p.107).

Quick and easy Chop ham and add it to any salad, or mix it with cheese and mayonnaise or fromage frais to make a filling for a baked potato.

ICE CREAM *(L)*

Recipes Basic: smoothie (p.69).

Quick and easy If your ice cream has melted, pour it over fruit salad, pie or crumbles, or use in a smoothie.

JUICES *(B)*

Recipes Individual: Fruit Juices (p.94).

Quick and easy Add leftover juice to some chopped fruit to make a fruit salad or use it on your cereal instead of milk.

Tip Make the juice when you have fruit that needs using up, then freeze it in 'portion' sizes so that they can be brought out of the freezer one at a time when required.

KIDNEY BEANS (CANNED) *(S)*

Recipes Basic: pie (pp.54-7), salad (p.62). Individual: Chilli con Carne (p.91).

Quick and easy Mix cooked beans with some cubed cucumber, tomato and red onion and a little vinaigrette for a really quick bean salad.

Tip Add canned kidney beans to a stew if you need to bulk it out.

LAMB *(C)*

Recipes Basic: curry (p.52), pie (p.55), risotto (p.59), rissoles (p.60), stir fry (p.74), stock (p.76). Individual: Lamb Pitta Pockets (p.97).

Quick and easy Cold, cooked lamb is delicious served with a baked potato and green salad. Try a little redcurrant jelly with your cold lamb.

Tips Cooked lamb should be cooled quickly and stored in the fridge or a cool place. Cover or wrap in aluminium foil to stop the meat from drying out.

LEEKS *(C/L)*

Recipes Basic: pie (p.57), quiche (p.58), risotto (p.59), roast vegetables (p.61), sauce (pp.65-66), soup (p.72), stir fry (p.74). Individual: Chicken Crunch (p.90).

Quick and easy Cooked leeks can be re-heated by tossing in hot melted butter in a saucepan.

Tip Even if the outer layers of the leek have dried out, just peel them off and the inner skin may still be fresh.

LEMONS *(O)*

Recipes Basic: stewed fruit (p.73). Individual: Lemon Vinaigrette (p.98).

Quick and easy Squeeze the juice of one lemon into a glass and add fizzy water and maybe a teaspoon of sugar for a really refreshing drink in summer.

Tips Squeeze lemon juice on cut vegetables and fruit to prevent discolouration. Add the zest to carrots or courgettes when cooking.

Can also be used in Banana and Chocolate Digestive Pudding (p.86), Bread and Butter Pudding (p.88), Fish Cakes (p.93), Fruit Juices (p.94).

See also Pancakes.

LENTILS *(L/S)*

Recipes Basic: soup (p.72). Individual: Quick Tomato and Lentil Soup (p.100), Vegetable Stew (p.106).

Tip Try mixing lentils with rice for extra flavour.

LIVER *(C)*

Quick and easy Leftover cooked liver can be made into pâté by putting it in a food processor with cooked onions, a pinch of thyme, black pepper and a spoonful of brandy. Process well until the pâté is smooth enough to spread on toast.

MANGE TOUT *(C/L)*

Recipes Basic: salad (p.62), stir fry (p.74).

Quick and easy Add leftover raw or cooked mange tout to a green salad.

MAYONNAISE *(L)*

Recipes Basic: salad (p.62). Individual: Baked Potato Fillings (p.84), Chicken Crunch (p.90).
Tip If you want to make a sandwich but there's only a tiny bit left in a big jar of mayonnaise, put your sandwich ingredients in the jar (e.g. tuna, cold chicken or tomatoes), put the lid on and shake. The ingredients will then be coated in mayonnaise ready for the sandwiches.
See also Bacon, Broad Beans, Chicken, Ham, Prawns.

MEAT *(C)*

See Beef, Lamb, Pork.

MELON *(L/O)*

Recipes Basic: fruit salad (p.53), smoothie (p.69). Individual: Fruit Juices (p.94).
Quick and easy Add chopped melon pieces to a green salad.
Tip If you have half a melon leftover, chop it into pieces and store them in an air tight container.

MILK *(O)*

Recipes Basic: quiche (p.58), sauce (p.66). Individual: Bread and Butter Pudding (p.88), Iced Coffee (p.96), Macaroni Cheese (p.99), Scones (p.102).
Tips Milk can be frozen but don't leave in the freezer for more than a month otherwise the milk may separate when it is thawed out. The last drops of milk in a carton can be used to brush over pastry on pies to make the pastry glossy when it's cooked. Slightly 'off' milk is ideal for scones.
Can also be used in Spanish Omelette (p.103), Welsh Rarebit (p.107).

MUSHROOMS *(L)*

Recipes Basic: crumble (p.51), pie (p.57), quiche (p.58), risotto (p.59), sauce (pp.65-6), stir fry (p.74), stock (p.78). Individual: Spanish Omelette (p.103), Vegetable Stew (p.106).
Quick and easy Fry sliced mushrooms in butter with a crushed clove of garlic. When soft, serve on hot buttered toast with cracked black pepper and parsley (optional).
Tip Add leftover mushrooms to the top of a pizza.

NUTS *(L)*

Recipe Basic: rissoles (p.60), salad (p.62).

Quick and easy Crushed nuts are ideal for sprinkling on top of cereal, yoghurt or fruit puddings.

Tip Beware of using nuts or nut oil as a 'hidden' ingredient if you are feeding someone who may have a nut allergy. Roasted nuts can be added to cooked vegetables to add extra taste.

ONIONS *(C/L)*

Recipes Basic: crumble (p.51), pie (pp.54-7), quiche (p.58), roast vegetables (p.61), salad (p.62), soup (p.72). Individual: Baked Potato Fillings (p.84), Bean and Onion Stew (p.87), Lamb Pitta Pockets (p.97), Sausage Special Fried Rice (p.101), Stuffed Peppers with Rice (p.104).

Quick and easy If you have half an onion leftover in the vegetable rack, slice it up and roast it with sausages in the oven. The juice from the sausages will add real substance to the onions. Serve leftover cooked onions with cold meat and chutney.

Tip Onions must be stored in a cool, dry place. If you've got some space, try hanging them in a breathable bag.

ORANGES *(L/O)*

Recipes Basic: fruit salad (p.53), smoothie (p.69). Individual: Bread and Butter Pudding (p.88), Fruit Juices (p.94).

Quick and easy Use the zest of an orange and a little butter to add flavour to carrots.

Tip Even when an orange seems to be soft, very often the juice will still be delicious so squeeze the orange juice and freeze if you're not using it straight away.

PANCAKES *(C)*

Tip If you have made too many pancakes, the leftovers can be frozen individually between layers of cling film and all wrapped in aluminium foil.

Quick and easy Pancakes can be stuffed with sweet or savoury fillings and are good for using up leftovers, e.g. cooked spinach and cheese sauce, or chopped banana with maple syrup and lemon juice.

PARSNIPS *(C/L)*

Recipes Basic: crumble (p.51), curry (p.52), pie (p.57), roast vegetables (p.61), soup (p.72), stock (p.78). Individual: Vegetable Stew (p.106).
Quick and easy Leftover roast parsnips are delicious fried as an alternative to chips.

PASTA *(C)*

Recipes Basic: salad (p.63). Individual: Macaroni Cheese (p.99).
Quick and easy Mix cold pasta with mayonnaise, tinned tuna and tinned sweet corn for a quick snack.

PEACHES *(L/O)*

Recipes Basic: crumble (p.50), fruit salad (p.53), smoothies (p.69) and stewed fruit (p.73). Individual: Fruit Juices (p.94).
Quick and easy If peaches are a little soft, slice them up, coat slices in sugar and place under a hot grill for 5-7 minutes. Serve with cream or crème fraîche.
Tip Peaches can often ripen and then go off very quickly. Try keeping them in the fridge and only bringing them out into the fruit bowl when they are going to be eaten.

PEARS *(L/O)*

Recipes Basic: crumble (p.50), fruit salad (p.53), smoothies (p.69), stewed fruit (p.73). Individual: Fruit Juices (p.94).
Quick and easy Core the pears and stuff with dried fruit. Bake in the oven for about 20-25 minutes, sitting the pears in shallow water to prevent them from drying out. You can also use this recipe for slightly soft apples.

PEAS *(C/L)*

Recipes Basic: pie (pp.54-7), quiche (p.58), risotto (p.59), salad (p.62), sauce (pp.64-6), soup (p.72). Individual: Fish Cakes (p.93), Macaroni Cheese (p.99), Sausage Special Fried Rice (p.101).
Quick and easy If you have a few frozen peas left in the packet, try them as a snack!
Tip Cold, cooked peas can be added to almost any dish to add colour and flavour.

PEPPERS *(C/L)*

Recipes Basic: crumble (p.51), quiche (p.58), risotto (p.59), roast vegetables (p.61), salad (p.62), soup (p.72), stir fry (p.74). Individual: Baked Potato Fillings (p.84), Chilli con Carne (p.91), Lamb Pitta Pockets (p.97), Stuffed Peppers with Rice (p.104), Vegetable Stew (p.106).

Quick and easy Slice up peppers lengthways and dip in houmous for a quick snack.

Tip Green, yellow and red peppers are a tasty addition to all the above and provide great flavour even if they appear a little wrinkly.

See also Potatoes, Rice.

PESTO

Recipes Individual: Quick Tomato and Lentil Soup (p.100).

Quick and easy Use it to add flavour to chicken sandwiches, or as the basis for a salad dressing (adding lemon juice and a little more oil if needed).

Tip Keep in fridge once opened.

See also Risotto (p.59).

PIE *(B)*

Recipes Basic: pie (pp.54-7).

Tip Leftover pie can be re-heated, but to avoid it being too dry, serve with a tomato sauce, leftover gravy or green salad with lots of dressing.

PLUMS *(L/O)*

Recipes Basic: crumble (p.50), fruit salad (p.53), smoothies (p.69) and stewed fruit (p.73).

Quick and easy Halve the plums and remove stones. Place in oven-proof dish, sprinkle with sugar and add a little water and sprinkle of ginger. Bake at 180°C for 20 minutes.

Tip Local plums, in season, are usually ready to eat, whereas plums from the supermarket may be very hard to ripen. To help ripen quickly put unripe fruit in a paper bag with a banana.

PORK (C)

Recipes Basic: curry (p.52), pie (p.55), risotto (p.59), rissoles (p.60), sauce (p.65).
Individual: Sausage Special Fried Rice (p.101).
Quick and easy Cold pork slices can be fried quickly on both sides and served with a green salad and pickle. Cold pork makes great sandwiches with either mustard or pickle.
See also Apricots, Stock.

POTATOES (C/L)

Recipes Basic: curry (p.52), pie (p.57), roast vegetables (p.61), salad (p.62), sauce (p.65), soup (p.72). Individual: Baked Cheesy Potatoes (p.83), Baked Potato Fillings (p.84), Spanish Omelette (p.103).
Quick and easy Cold roast or baked potatoes can be sliced up and fried in oil with onions – add cooked French beans or red peppers to make a tasty snack. Cold mashed potato can be mixed with grated cheese, rolled into croquettes and fried, or used to top a pie.
Tip Store potatoes in a dark, cool place.

POULTRY (C)

Recipes Basic: poultry stock (p.77). Individual: Chicken Crunch (p.90).
Tip Store cold chicken or turkey in an airtight container or freeze it to use later.
See also Chicken, Turkey.

PRAWNS (C)

Recipes Basic: curry (p.52), risotto (p.59), salad (p.62).
Quick and easy Prawn and mayonnaise sandwich – the most popular selling sandwich in the UK – not without reason! Add a squeeze of lemon juice to the mayonnaise.
Tip Prawns do not last in the fridge for more than about three days, so plan ahead!

QUICHE (B)

Recipe Basic: quiche (p.58).
Tip Leftover quiche can be re-heated but to avoid it being too dry, serve with a green salad with lots of dressing.

RASPBERRIES *(L/O)*

Recipes Basic: crumble (p.50), fruit salad (p.53), smoothies (p.69). Individual: Fruit Juices (p.94), Summer Pudding (p.105).

Quick and easy If raspberries are past their best, put them in a juicer and process until smooth. Sieve the juice to remove the pips. Pour over vanilla ice cream.

Tip Freeze raspberries on a tray, and transfer frozen berries into a freezer bag.

RHUBARB *(C)*

Recipes Basic: crumble (p.50), stewed fruit (p.73).

Quick and easy Leftover cooked rhubarb is delicious on breakfast cereal, or mix with natural yoghurt to make instant rhubarb fool.

Tip Add powdered ginger or slices of stemmed ginger to rhubarb when stewing or baking.

RICE *(C)*

Recipes Basic: salad (p.62), stir fry (p.74). Individual: Sausage Special Fried Rice (p.101), Stuffed Peppers with Rice (p.104).

Quick and easy Add any combination of chopped tomato, red onion, peppers, spring onion, cucumber and sultanas to the cold, cooked rice with a tablespoon of lemon juice and olive oil for a quick rice salad.

Tip Freeze cooked rice in self-sealing plastic bags in portions. To re-heat add 2 tablespoons of liquid (water/stock) and microwave at 100% power for 2 minutes, or heat in a saucepan over a high heat – stirring constantly. Make sure the rice is heated right through before serving. For safety always cool cooked rice quickly and refrigerate as soon as possible.

See also Couscous, Cucumber, Lentils, Onions.

RISOTTO *(B)*

Recipe Basic: risotto (p.59).

Tip Leftover risotto can be re-heated but make sure you do it thoroughly.

RISSOLES *(B)*
Recipe Basic: rissoles (p.60).
Tip Leftover rissoles can be crumbled into a pasta sauce or shepherds pie.

ROAST VEGETABLES *(B)*
Recipe Basic: roast vegetables (p.61), soup (p.72). Individual: Baked Potato Fillings (p.84), Lamb Pitta Pockets (p.97), Macaroni Cheese (p.99).
Quick and easy Cold roast vegetables and houmous, with cracked black pepper make a delicious quick sandwich. Add cold roast vegetables into a salad, with some olive oil, to add a Mediterranean flavour.

RUNNER BEANS *(C/L)*
Recipes Basic: curry (p.52), salad (p.62), soup (p.72), stir fry (p.74).
Tip Runner beans grow very well in this country so there is often a glut in summer which is a good time to buy them and freeze them for later in the year: 'blanche' the chopped and pre-pared beans by placing them in boiling water for 2 minutes. Drain fully on kitchen paper and transfer into a freezer bag. Cool and freeze immediately.

SAUCE *(B)*
Recipes Basic: brown, tomato and white sauces (pp.64-6).
Tips The addition of a sauce, fresh or re-heated, can turn leftover meat, poultry or vegetables into a delicious snack or meal.

SAUSAGES *(C)*
Recipes pie (p.55), risotto (p.59), sauce (p.65). Individual: Sausage Special Fried Rice (p.101).
Quick and easy leftover cold sausages are ideal for a quick snack, either dipped in mustard sauce or between fresh bread for a sausage sandwich. They're also ideal for picnics.
See also Onions.

SMOOTHIE *(B)*

Recipe Basic: smoothie (p.69).

Tip Any leftover smoothie can be poured into a lollie mould to make iced smoothie lollies.

SOUP *(L/O)*

Recipe Basic: soup (p.72).

SPINACH *(C)*

Recipe Basic: quiche (p.58).

Quick and easy Eggs and spinach bake: spread the cooked spinach in an oven-proof dish and cover with cheese sauce (see p.66) and chopped-up hard boiled eggs. Cook until golden brown.

STIR FRY *(B)*

Recipe Basic: stir fry (p.74).

Tip Leftover stir fry can be re-heated by microwaving for 60 seconds or heating for 5 minutes in a wok or frying pan, stirring continuously.

STOCK *(B)*

Recipes Basic: pie (pp.54-7), risotto (p.59), sauce (p.64-5), soup (p.72), stock (pp.75-8).

Tips Use leftover stock instead of water when cooking rice to add extra flavour. Stock freezes well so make your stock when you have a meat, poultry or fish carcass available and freeze to use for another time. A good strong stock, made from meat or fish bones or poultry carcasses provides the ideal basis for making soup, a sauce or stews, adding extra flavour and substance.

STRAWBERRIES *(L/O)*

Recipes Basic: fruit salad (p.53), smoothie (p.69). Individual: Fruit Juices (p.94), Summer Pudding (p.105).

Quick and easy Slice up strawberries and serve on top of muesli or breakfast cereal with a dollop of yoghurt.

SWEDE *(C/L)*

Recipes Basic: crumble (p.51), curry (p.52), pie (p.57), roast vegetables (p.61), soup (p.72), stock (p.78).

Quick and easy Fry leftover, mashed swede in butter to make a crispy swede pancake. Serve with lots of black pepper.

SWEET POTATO *(C/L)*

Recipes Basic: crumble (p.51), curry (p.52), pie (p.57), roast vegetables (p.61), soup (p.72).

Quick and easy Bake the sweet potato in the oven for 40-45 minutes and serve with a wedge of butter, grated parmesan and parsley.

SWEET CORN *(C/S)*

Recipes Basic: crumble (p.51), pie (p.57), risotto (p.59), salad (p.62). Individual: Baked Potato Fillings (p.84), Bubble and Squeak (p.89), Macaroni Cheese (p.99), Sausage Special Fried Rice (p.101).

Quick and easy Mix up some tinned sweet corn with any leftover chicken or turkey meat and a tablespoon of mayonnaise for a delicious sandwich or baked potato filling.

TOMATO *(L/S)*

Recipes Basic: crumble (p.51), curry (p.52), pie (p.57), quiche (p.58), risotto (p.59), roast vegetables (p.61), salad (p.62), sauce (p.65), soup (p.72). Individual: Bean and Onion Stew (p.87), Macaroni Cheese (p.99), Quick Tomato and Lentil Soup (p.100), Stuffed Peppers with Rice (p.104), Vegetable Stew (p.106).

Quick and easy Chop up any slightly soft tomatoes in a food processor with half an onion and 1 small chilli (optional) and some lemon juice, to make a delicious salsa. Serve with tortilla chips or as a side serving at barbecues.

Tip Keep a few tins of chopped tomatoes in the cupboard for quick pasta sauce.

See also Kidney Beans (canned), Rice.

TUNA *(S)*

Recipes Basic: sauce (p.65). Individual: Baked Potato Fillings (p.84), Fish Cakes (p.93).

Quick and easy Add it to mayonnaise, some chopped-up spring onion and sweet corn to make a delicious sandwich or panini.

Tip Once a tin is opened, transfer any unused tuna into a plastic container or bowl covered with clingfilm.

TURKEY *(C)*

Recipes Basic: curry (p.52), pie (p.54), risotto (p.59), rissoles (p.60), stir fry (p.74), stock (p.77). Individual: Chicken Crunch (p.90).

Quick and easy Cold turkey and cranberry sauce sandwiches.

Tip If you have a lot of turkey meat leftover after Christmas, freeze it in portions so that it can be used when needed.

See also Chicken, Poultry.

VEGETABLES *(L/C)*

Recipes Basic: crumble (p.51), pie (p.57), soup (p.72), stir fry (p.74). Individual: Vegetable Stew (p.106).

Tips Vegetables still contain a good deal of flavour even when a bit wrinkly and dried out – soups and pies are ideal for using up vegetables left in the rack. Vegetables will keep fresh for much longer by wrapping in wet newspaper and storing in a plastic bag in the fridge.

See also individual vegetables, e.g. Broad Beans.

YOGHURT *(L)*

Recipes Individual: Banana and Chocolate Digestive Pudding (p.86).

Quick and easy Yoghurt makes a wonderful snack with a spoonful of honey and some chopped banana or nuts.

Tips A dollop of natural yoghurt is great on a hot curry, to cool it down, or on any fruit pudding. A spoonful of natural yoghurt can be added to mayonnaise to thin it – ideal for making a chicken or tuna sandwich or potato salad.

See also cucumber and individual fruits, e.g. strawberries.

Basic recipes

that can be adapted for different leftovers

Basic CRUMBLE – FRUIT

 15 40

Suitable for

Cooked or leftover apples • apricots • blackberries • blackcurrants • blueberries • cherries • peaches • pears • plums • rhubarb

Ingredients

- 300 – 400g chopped, cored and peeled fruit
- ½ lemon squeezed
- Sugar (few spoonfuls, more if using cooking apples or sour fruit)
- Jam/honey as an alternative to sugar

For topping

- 200g plain flour or a combination of 200g of a combination of flour and oats, flour and muesli, flour and crumbled biscuits
- 75g butter at room temperature
- 75g soft brown or caster sugar

Method

1. Pre-heat oven to 170°C/340°F/Gas mark 4
2. Layer the fruit in the bowl (sprinkle each layer with sugar or dollops of jam/honey)
3. Put the flour and butter into mixing bowl and rub together with your fingers until it looks like breadcrumbs. Add sugar and combine
4. Sprinkle the entire crumble ingredients on top of the fruit and cook in the oven for 40 minutes or until crumble has turned golden brown. To make a pie, instead of crumble you can use shortcrust pastry. Roll out, lay over the fruit and cook for 35 minutes
5. Serve hot with cream, crème fraîche, custard or ice cream (or even melted ice cream)

Basic **CRUMBLE – VEGETABLE**

 10 75

Suitable for

For winter vegetable crumble: carrots • parsnips • swede • sweet potato • turnips • leeks • broccoli • cabbage. *For summer vegetable crumble:* courgettes • red peppers • aubergine • tomatoes.

Ingredients

- Approx 400g of a combination of the above vegetables (raw)
- 2 onions
- 25g margarine or butter
- 1 tablespoon flour
- 300ml vegetable stock
- 30ml tomato purée
- 30ml horseradish sauce (optional)
- For topping 200g plain flour or 200g of a combination of flour and oats
- 75g butter

Method

1. Pre-heat oven to 170°C/340°F/Gas mark 4
2. Dice or chop the vegetables, slice the onion and melt the butter in a casserole dish, fry the chopped onion for about 3 minutes until soft. Stir in the flour, removing as many lumps as possible gradually adding in the stock stirring all the time until you have a smooth sauce
3. Add the chopped vegetables, tomato purée and horseradish sauce, if using salt and pepper, cover with a lid and place in the oven for 45 minutes
4. Transfer the mixture to a large pie dish
5. For the topping, put the flour or combination of flour and oats in a bowl and chop up the butter into the flour
6. Using your hands, gradually blend the butter into the flour until it is evenly distributed and the mixture looks like breadcrumbs
7. Scatter topping over vegetables and bake for 30 minutes

Basic **CURRY**

 10 15

Suitable for

Bite-sized pieces of cooked or raw chicken, turkey, pork or beef
• cooked or raw vegetables: carrots, cauliflower, French beans, peppers,
tomatoes • cooked potatoes.

Ingredients

- Roughly 500g of any of the above
- 4 tablespoons olive or sesame oil
- 1 onion, chopped
- 2 cloves garlic, crushed
- ¼ teaspoon salt
- 1 teaspoon curry powder
- ½ green chilli, chopped and de-seeded (or adjust according to taste)
- 1 tablespoon tomato purée
- 30ml double cream or crème fraîche (optional)

Method

1. Heat the oil over a high heat in a wok or frying pan. Add the onion and fry for a couple of minutes. Then add the garlic
2. Add any raw meat (around 400g). Cook for a further 5 minutes if using raw meat. Skip this if using cooked meat
3. Add any raw vegetables and cook for 5 minutes, stirring all the time. Skip this if using cooked vegetables
4. Add the curry powder and chilli. Stir well.
5. Add cooked meat and vegetables and stir well to ensure they are coated in the curry powder
6. Add tomato purée. Stir the ingredients well for 5 mins to ensure all spices are absorbed
7. Just before serving, add the double cream if using, and mix in well. Garnish with fresh coriander leaves

Basic **FRUIT SALAD**

 10

Suitable for

Raw: oranges · apples · apricots · melon · grapes · strawberries
· raspberries · blackberries · blackcurrants · bananas · blueberries
· kiwi fruit · pears · peaches · tangerines · satsumas · lychees · pineapple
· tinned fruit such as pineapple or peaches.

Ingredients

* 500g of any of the above fruit
* 200ml water with 2 tablespoons sugar or juice from a 400g tin of fruit with 100ml orange juice or water.

Method

1. Peel, core/de-seed and chop all the fruit, except bananas, into bite-sized pieces and mix in a large bowl. Bananas discolour very quickly so add them when you are about to serve up. Sprinkling a little lemon juice on the fruit salad will help prevent discolouration.

2. For the juice:
   · *either* put 200ml of water in a saucepan and add 2 tablespoons of sugar. Bring to the boil and stir until all the sugar has melted. Allow to cool and add to the fruit in the bowl
   · *or* use the juice from a tin of fruit and add a little water or orange juice

3. Cover the bowl in cling film, allow to cool if necessary before storing in the fridge. Serve with cream, crème fraîche or yoghurt

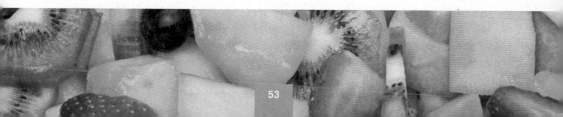

Basic **PIE – CHICKEN**

 15   45

Suitable for

Cooked chicken or turkey • cooked gammon ham or bacon • cooked or raw carrots, leeks, peas, sweet corn, mushrooms • chicken or turkey gravy.

Ingredients

- About 500g cooked chicken or turkey
- About 150g bacon or ham cubed (optional)
- 1 onion, chopped, 1 or 2 leeks, chopped
- 3 carrots, chopped, leftover peas, small tin of sweet corn (optional)
- 200g mushrooms (optional), 500ml (750g if not using milk) stock – see p.77
- 250ml milk (optional), 100ml white wine (optional)
- Salt and pepper, tarragon (optional)
- 2 tablespoons flour, 50g butter
- Packet of frozen short crust pastry/4 servings of mashed potato

Method

❶ Make sure pastry is completely defrosted. Pre-heat the oven to 180°C/350°F/Gas mark 4

❷ Fry up the bacon pieces, if using, for 3 minutes. Add the onion and cook for a further 2 minutes. Add the raw vegetables and cook for 2 minutes. Add the flour and mix in to remove as many lumps as possible

❸ Gradually blend in the stock/milk (and wine if you are using it), stirring constantly over a medium heat until the sauce becomes thick and smooth.

❹ Stir in any leftover cooked vegetables and cooked chicken or turkey, season and transfer to an oven-proof pie dish

❺ Roll out the pastry a little larger than the dish, cover the dish with the pastry and press down around the lip of the dish. Dampen the edges so they stick down well. Pierce a hole in the top to allow steam to escape. Alternatively, add a topping of mashed potato

❻ For pastry, cook pie in the oven for 35 minutes – until the pastry is cooked. If using mashed potatoes, cook for 20 minutes until potato turns golden

Basic PIE – MEAT

⏱ 15 ⏱ 45

Suitable for

Leftover cooked beef, pork, gammon, ham or sausage, cubed • raw or cooked carrots, parsnips or swede.

Ingredients

- About 500g cooked meat, plus 50g butter
- 1 onion, chopped, 1 clove garlic
- 1 tablespoon flour
- 1 pint (brown) stock – see p.76
- ½ glass red wine/1 glass beer or wine (optional)
- Worcestershire sauce, salt and pepper
- Packet of frozen short crust pastry or about 5 large boiled potatoes
  Plus any of the following:
  Tinned chopped tomatoes • raw or cooked chopped vegetables e.g. carrots, parsnips, swede

Method

❶ Make sure pastry is completely defrosted. Pre-heat the oven to 180°/350°F/Gas mark 4.

❷ Melt the butter in a casserole dish. Fry the chopped onion and garlic for about 3 minutes until soft. Add the raw vegetables and fry for a further 2 minutes

❸ Stir in the flour, removing as many lumps as possible. Gradually add the stock and red wine or beer, stirring all the time until the sauce becomes thick and smooth

❹ Stir in cooked meat, tinned tomatoes and any cooked vegetables. Add salt and pepper and transfer to an oven-proof pie dish

❺ Roll out the pastry a little larger than the dish, cover the dish with the pastry and press down around the lip of the dish. Dampen the edges so they stick down well. Pierce a hole in the top to allow steam to escape. Alternatively, finely slice some cold cooked potatoes and lay them on top of the meat.

❻ Glaze with some melted butter or milk

❼ For pastry, cook pie in the oven for 35 minutes – until the pastry is cooked. If using potatoes, cook for 20 minutes

Basic PIE – SHEPHERD'S / COTTAGE ⏱ 20 ⏱ 45

Traditionally, beef is used in a cottage pie and lamb is used in a shepherd's pie.

Suitable for

Cooked, minced (or finely chopped) lamb or beef • cooked or raw carrots • leftover mashed potato

Ingredients

- leftover roast joint of lamb or beef, minced or cut into small pieces
- 4 carrots (leftovers or raw) chopped
- 1 large onion finely chopped
- ½ pint of stock – see p.76 – and/or gravy
- 2 tablespoons vegetable oil
- 1 kg mashed potato (or raw potatoes to mash) or chopped-up leftover roast potatoes

Method

1. Pre-heat the oven to 180°/350°F/Gas mark 4
2. If you are making mashed potato, peel and cut potatoes into uniform sizes and boil in salted water for up to 15 minutes, depending on the size of the potatoes
3. When the potatoes are soft enough to mash, drain thoroughly. Mash with the butter and a dash of full fat milk. Add a little salt and pepper
4. Meanwhile, fry the onions in the oil until they are just turning golden but not burnt
5. Add the mince and carrots and stir until the mixture is heated through – if you are using raw carrots, don't worry that the carrots aren't soft yet. Add the stock/gravy and transfer to an oven-proof pie dish
6. Spread the mashed potato, or chopped-up leftover roast potatoes evenly over the meat in the dish
7. Bake in oven for at least 20 minutes, until the potato is golden, and serve immediately

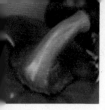

Basic **PIE – VEGETABLE**

Suitable for

For winter pie: carrots • parsnips • swede • sweet potato • turnips • leeks • green beans • broccoli • cabbage.
For summer pie: courgettes • red peppers • aubergine • tomatoes

Ingredients

- About 500g combination of raw vegetables as above
- 2 onions
- 25g margarine
- 550ml vegetable stock – see p.78
- 30ml tomato purée
- 30ml horseradish sauce
- 1 packet frozen short crust pastry or 5 large cooked potatoes

Method

1. Make sure pastry is completely defrosted
2. Pre-heat oven to 170°C/340°F/Gas mark 4
3. Dice or chop the vegetables. Slice the onion
4. Melt the margarine in a casserole dish, stir in all the vegetables, cover and sweat for 10 minutes
5. Pour in stock and bring to the boil, add tomato purée and horseradish sauce.
6. Cover and put in oven for 20-25 minutes
7. Transfer to a large pie dish
8. Roll out the pastry a little larger than the dish, cover the dish with the pastry and press down around the lip of the dish. Dampen the edges so they stick down well. Pierce a hole in the top to allow steam to escape. Alternatively you can use sliced up cooked potatoes to cover the pie
9. For pastry, cook pie in the oven for 35 minutes – until the pastry is cooked. If using potatoes, cook for 20 minutes

Basic **QUICHE**

⏱ 10 ⏱ 30

The beauty of quiches is that they are perfect for using up virtually any combination of leftover meat and vegetables, and can be eaten cold or hot. Some really good combinations include cooked salmon and broccoli (or leek), chicken and vegetable or ham and mushroom.

Suitable for

Cooked, chopped bacon bits • cooked and sliced mushrooms • cooked broccoli, leeks, spinach or peas • diced ham • cooked chopped onion • cheese • salmon

Ingredients

- 1 packet of frozen short crust pastry or 1 x 25cm short crust pastry case, pre-cooked
- 60g grated cheese
- 2 eggs plus 2 egg yolks
- 250ml milk
- 125ml double cream (optional)
- Salt and pepper to taste
- Pinch grated nutmeg

Method

1. Pre-heat the oven to 190°C/375°F/gas mark 5
2. Defrost frozen pastry fully if using, and roll out a little larger than the flan dish. Line the dish with the pastry down, pushing it down so it sticks to the rim and sides. Cut the excess pastry off
3. Use a fork to make some holes in the base and cook for 15 minutes. Alternatively, use a pre-cooked pastry case placed on an oven tray
4. Spread your leftover ingredients evenly on the pastry
5. Put the eggs, egg yolks, milk, cream (if using), salt and pepper and nutmeg in a bowl and whisk together well. If not using cream, then add extra milk instead
6. Pour over the ingredients inside the flan case. Season with salt and pepper
7. Bake in the oven for about 25-30 minutes until the quiche mixture has set and slightly browned on the top

Basic **RISOTTO**

 10 30

While you can use all kinds of cooked or raw leftovers in risotto, it is best to use uncooked rice, as the flavours are absorbed by the rice during the cooking process.

Suitable for

Cooked or raw peas, broccoli, leeks • mushrooms • cooked meat or poultry • cooked ham or gammon • raw or cooked bacon • cooked prawns

Ingredients

- 350 g Arborio or other short-grain Italian rice
- 1 onion finely chopped
- 1 or 2 garlic cloves crushed
- 1 litre vegetable or chicken stock
- Glass of white wine (optional), grated Parmesan
- 2 tbsps olive oil, a squeeze of lemon

Method

❶ Heat up the stock in a saucepan. Allow it to simmer with lid on to keep it from evaporating.

❷ Heat olive oil in large saucepan, add onions and fry gently until soft but not coloured. Add garlic and any raw bacon and continue to cook for a 1 minute or so

❸ Add the rice and stir until coated with oil. Let it cook for 1 minute, being careful not to let it burn

❹ Add the wine, if using, then turn heat right down and let it simmer until wine has been absorbed, stirring all the time

❺ Add a couple of ladles of stock, stir, and continue simmering until the stock has been absorbed

❻ Repeat this until you have finished the stock. The rice should be cooked by now, firm and glossy but not sticky

❼ Add a handful of parmesan and stir it round and serve, or add a squeeze of lemon or a dollop of pesto on each serving with some cracked, black pepper and a bit more parmesan

Basic **RISSOLES**

🕐 15 🕐 10-15

Rissoles are an old-fashioned dish, but were invented for a reason – to use up leftover meat and poultry in a way that was quick, easy and inexpensive, using only staple, store cupboard ingredients. The vegetarian option, using nuts, is also delicious.

Suitable for

Cooked beef · lamb · pork · chicken or turkey · nuts

Ingredients

- 225g cooked, mixed or finely chopped meat or poultry or unsalted, finely chopped mixed nuts
- 1 onion, finely chopped
- 50g breadcrumbs – see p.27
- 2 teaspoons chopped fresh or dried parsley
- 1 teaspoon fresh or dried rosemary
- 1 clove garlic, crushed
- 1 teaspoon tomato purée
- 1 teaspoon Tabasco sauce (optional)
- 1 egg, beaten
- Flour, seasoned with salt and pepper
- 2 tablespoons of vegetable or olive oil
- Salt and pepper to taste

Method

❶ Mix all the ingredients (except the flour and oil) in a large bowl
❷ Divide up the mixture into 8 and roll into balls
❸ Roll each ball in the seasoned flour
❹ Heat the oil in a frying pan over a medium heat. When the oil is hot, add the rissoles and fry for about 10 minutes, turning occasionally, until golden-brown all over and cooked
❺ Serve immediately

Basic **ROAST VEGETABLES**

 10 25

This is a fabulous way of using up any vegetables that need to be eaten. You can use some or all of the ingredients, depending on the vegetables you have available and what is in season at the time. The more variety of vegetables the better the taste.

Suitable for

Raw: parsnips • aubergine • butternut squash • swede • leeks • carrots • courgettes • red/yellow peppers • mushrooms • potatoes • cherry tomatoes • French beans • baby corn

Ingredients

- 2 red or white onions
- 3 cloves garlic
- 500g mixture of the above vegetables
- 2 sprigs of rosemary
- 3 sprigs thyme
- Salt and pepper
- 2 big slugs of olive or vegetable oil

Method

1. Pre-heat the oven to 200°C/400°F/gas mark 6
2. Roughly chop vegetables making sure that those which take longer to cook – such as potatoes, butternut squash, sweet potato, swede and parsnips – are smallest, to ensure that all vegetables will be ready at the same time
3. Put all the vegetables in a large baking tray and cover with the rosemary and thyme.
4. Pour the oil over the vegetables
5. Use your hands (clean!) to stir up the vegetables to make sure they are all coated in the oil and space evenly in the baking tray
6. Cook in the oven for 25 minutes. After about 10 minutes, take the tray out and stir the vegetables to make sure they all cook evenly
7. Try serving with chopped-up feta cheese mixed in

Basic **SALAD**

 5

There are many varieties and combinations of salad possible, and whilst the ingredients of the salad are important, the dressing makes all the difference. Here are a few suggestions for salads and the dressings to serve with them.

Waldorf (Apple and Celery) Salad

Suitable for

Raw apples, celery, walnuts and raisins.

Method

1. Dice up some apple and celery and add chopped walnuts and raisins. Mix with a dressing of mayonnaise, lemon juice and black pepper, and serve immediately or store in a sealed container to stop the apple going brown

Easy potato salad

Suitable for

Cooked boiled potatoes.

Method

1. Cut the potatoes into bite-sized chunks. Mix with chopped chives and a dressing of a crushed clove of garlic, lemon juice, Dijon mustard and tarragon

Rice salad

Suitable for

Cooked rice or couscous.

Method

1. Add chopped tomatoes, red peppers, cucumber, raisins and chopped walnuts to the rice, and mix with Lemon vinaigrette (p.98)

Pasta salad

Suitable for

Cooked pasta (except lasagne, spaghetti and tagliatelle).

Method

❶ Combine the cold, cooked pasta with any of the following: halved cherry tomatoes, cubed cucumber, finely chopped raw red onion, shredded raw red cabbage and chopped raw red pepper

❷ Serve with Lemon vinaigrette (p.98) or a dressing of mayonnaise, lemon juice and black pepper

French bean salad

Suitable for

Cooked French beans.

Method

❶ For the dressing: fry 3 cloves of sliced garlic in a tablespoon of olive oil until crisp and golden. Cool, then add 2 more tablespoons of olive oil, 1 tablespoon of balsamic vinegar and 3 tablespoons of chopped-up mint.

❷ Toss beans in the dressing until well coated, season and serve

Three bean salad

Suitable for

Canned or cooked beans (e.g. kidney, borlotti or butter beans).

Method

❶ Finely chop an onion, mix with the beans and chopped tomatoes (optional), and coat in Lemon vinaigrette (p.98)

Basic SAUCE – BROWN (GRAVY) 🕐 5 🕐 10

This can be used as a gravy with meat or
vegetables, or combined with cooked meat or poultry in a pie.

Ingredients

- 50g butter
- 1 onion, chopped
- 1 clove garlic
- 1 tablespoon flour
- 1 pint meat stock
- ½ glass red wine/1 glass beer (optional)
- Salt and pepper

Method

1. Melt the butter in a saucepan
2. Fry the chopped onion for about 3 minutes until soft
3. Add the garlic and fry for a further 2 minutes
4. Blend in the flour, removing as many lumps as possible
5. Add the stock and red wine or beer bit by bit stirring all the time
6. The sauce is then ready to be used for pies and stews

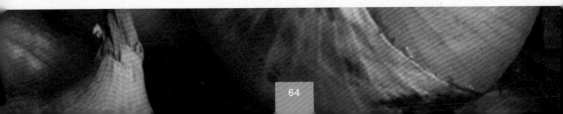

Basic **SAUCE – TOMATO**

🕐 5 🕐 20

A basic tomato sauce can be used to make any pasta or rice meal, either on its own or with the addition of other leftover ingredients.

Ingredients

- 1 tablespoon of olive oil
- 1 onion, chopped
- 1 clove garlic, chopped
- 1 x 400g can of chopped tomatoes or 4 large tomatoes
- Salt and black pepper
- 8 basil leaves or 1 teaspoon dried basil
- Grated Parmesan to taste

Plus any of the following:

Cooked chicken, turkey, pork or beef, chopped or minced • cooked sausage, salami, ham, bacon or chorizo, sliced • tuna • sweet corn • mushrooms • tomatoes • courgettes, chopped • leeks, chopped • peas • broccoli

Method

1 Heat the oil in a saucepan or frying pan and add the onion and garlic
2 Cook for about 3 minutes until the onion and garlic are soft, add some salt and pepper
3 Add any raw vegetables, chopped and cook for 4 minutes stirring continually
4 Add the tinned tomatoes and stir in
5 Add any of the cooked meat or vegetables and heat through for about 10 minutes
6 Add the basil leaves, chopped, or the dried basil
7 Serve with any types of pasta

Basic **SAUCE – WHITE**

🕐 2 🕐 5

Variations of white sauce can be used with all kinds of cooked vegetables, such as broccoli, cauliflower and leeks, and with cooked poultry or ham, e.g. in a pie.

Ingredients

- 50g butter
- 2 tablespoons flour
- 250ml milk
- Salt and pepper
- ½ teaspoon grainy mustard (optional)

Method

1. Melt the butter in a saucepan.
2. Add the flour and mix well until butter and flour form a ball and leave the sides of the pan – do not allow to go brown.
3. Gradually blend in the milk, stirring constantly over a medium heat until the sauce becomes thick and smooth.
4. Bring to the boil and cook for 1-2 minutes, stirring all the time. Season with salt and pepper.

White sauce variations:

Cheese sauce	Add 50g cheddar cheese
Parsley sauce	Add 2 tablespoons finely chopped parsley
Mushroom sauce	Cook 100g thinly sliced mushrooms in melted butter until soft and add to the sauce
Egg and mustard sauce	Finely chop three hardboiled eggs and add them to the sauce, along with 1 teaspoon of English mustard
Rich white sauce	Whisk 1 egg yolk with 2 tablespoons of cream and then mix into the white sauce

Basic **SMOOTHIE**

 5

Smoothies are the most fantastic way of using up soft fruit that is beginning to look a little weary. The use of bananas in a number of smoothie recipes makes them thicker than juices. For an extra creamy smoothie, add a dollop of ice cream.

Suitable for

Leftover or over-ripe fruit.

Method for all smoothies

Put all the ingredients into a blender and mix for about 1 minute

'Pink Banana'

Ingredients

- 1 banana
- Handful of strawberries or raspberries (tinned, frozen or fresh)
- 1 large glass of apple juice

'Classic Banana'

Ingredients

- 2 large bananas
- One ripe peach (stoned and peeled)
- Seeds and pulp of one passion fruit
- 1 teaspoon honey

Tip Try freezing the bananas first for a really creamy smoothie!

'Rare Pear'

Ingredients

- 2 pears (pealed and cored) or one tin of pear halves in fruit juice
- 1 banana
- 1 tin of mandarin pieces
- A dash of lime or lemon juice

Tip pears are easily bruised but that doesn't mean they can't be used. Just cut around the bruised area and use the rest – it will still be delicious.

'Ruby Red'

Ingredients

3 large handfuls of raspberries or a packet of frozen raspberries
200ml cranberry juice
2 bananas
Tip pour this over some ice cream for a really delicious dessert.

'Strawberry Slush'

Ingredients

- 2 handfuls of strawberries (stalks removed)
- 1 banana
- Juice of one orange or 150ml of orange juice

Tip add some ice before blending to get a crushed ice smoothie.

'Appleberry Finn'

Ingredients

- 2 handfuls of strawberries
- 1 large glass of apple juice
- 1 banana

'Black 'n' Blueberry'

Ingredients

- 2 handfuls of blueberries (fresh, frozen or tinned)
- 2 handfuls of blackcurrants (fresh, frozen or tinned)
- 1 teaspoon honey
- 5 ice cubes

'Belting Blueberry'

Ingredients

- 2 handfuls blueberries (fresh, frozen or tinned)
- 1 glass orange juice
- Six fresh strawberries
- 1 banana

Basic **SOUP**

🕐 5   🕐 15

Small amounts of leftover fish, meat, poultry and vegetables can quickly be made into a satisfying soup, and the addition of a good strong stock can make all the difference to the taste. Ideally, use chicken stock for chicken soup, meat stock for a meat-based soup etc. However, chicken stock for a vegetable soup is fine as long as it is supplemented with plenty of strong-tasting vegetables.

Suitable for

Leftover cooked fish, meat, poultry and any vegetables.

Ingredients

- 25g butter
- 1 onion, diced
- 1 small potato, diced
- 1 teaspoon curry powder (optional)
- Salt and pepper to taste
- 1 litre of stock (or equivalent stock from stock cubes) – see pp.75-8

Plus whichever leftovers you want to use up.

Method

1. Melt the butter in a saucepan and fry the onion, potato and any raw vegetables you want to use gently for 5 minutes
2. Add the curry powder, if using, and cook for 5 minutes, stirring continually
3. Add the stock, leftover meat, poultry or cooked vegetables and salt and pepper
4. Simmer for 10 minutes
5. Liquidise if you like a smooth soup
6. Serve garnished with parsley or coriander

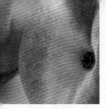

Basic **STEWED FRUIT**

 10 15

Stewed fruit is a delicious pudding on its own, or makes the base of a fruit crumble or pie. Try serving stewed fruit on top of vanilla ice cream or with hot custard.

Suitable for

All kinds of raw fruit: apples • apricots • blackberries • blackcurrants • blueberries • peaches • pears • plums • rhubarb.

Ingredients

- 400g fruit (cored, peeled or de-seeded and chopped/quartered as necessary)
- 125g sugar
- 3 pieces of lemon peel
- 1 clove (optional)
- 1 cinnamon stick (optional)
- 1 vanilla pod (optional)
- 200ml water

Method

1. Put all the ingredients in a wide-bottomed saucepan and bring to the boil
2. Turn down the heat and let the fruit simmer for another 10 minutes
3. Take off the heat and allow to cool
4. Remove the cinnamon stick, vanilla pod and clove using a slotted spoon
5. Serve or, if using in a crumble see p.50, or pie see p.57

Basic STIR FRY

🕐 10 🕐 15-20

This is ideal for lone vegetables left in the rack.
Cooked vegetables, such as carrots, mange tout or peppers can be used, but for best results use raw vegetables.

Suitable for

Cooked or raw meat, poultry or prawns • cooked or raw vegetables: carrots, broccoli, bean sprouts, mange tout, French beans, red peppers, yellow peppers, mushrooms, leeks, courgettes, celery, cauliflower, spring onions, lemon juice

Ingredients

- 400g of any mixture of the above ingredients (chopped or sliced)
- 1cm fresh grated ginger (optional)
- 2 tablespoons sesame oil (or vegetable oil)
- 2 tablespoons dark Soy sauce
- Any leftover cold rice (optional)
- 1 fresh chilli, chopped (optional)

Method

1. Heat the oil over a high heat in a wok or frying pan
2. If time, marinate any uncooked ingredients in Soy sauce for a few hours before cooking
3. Add any uncooked meat, poultry or prawns, plus ginger if you are using it, and fry for about 3 minutes, stirring constantly
4. Add vegetables and fry for a further 10 minutes, tossing the vegetables all the time. To add some bite to the stir fry, add 1 finely chopped chilli with to vegetables
5. Add any cooked meat, poultry or prawns and any cold, cooked rice and carry on stir frying until these are heated thoroughly (about 3-4 minutes)
6. Add the Soy sauce and stir so that it is well mixed in
7. Serve immediately

Basic STOCK – FISH

⏱ 10 ⏱ 45

Suitable for

Fish bones.

Ingredients

- 2lb fish bones
- 1 onion, cut in quarters
- Pinch of parsley
- Pinch of thyme
- Bay leaf
- 1 teaspoon lemon juice
- 500-1000ml water
- Salt and pepper

Method

1. Put all the ingredients in a large pan and season well with salt and pepper.
2. Bring stock to the boil, skim off any scum from the surface, cover and simmer for 30-45 minutes
3. Strain through fine sieve and cool
4. Fish stock can be frozen but should not be kept in the fridge for more than 48 hours before using

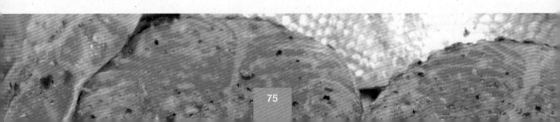

Basic **STOCK – MEAT**

🕐 10 🕐 60+

Suitable for

Leftover meat bones, scraps of meat and leftover vegetables.

Ingredients

- Stripped carcass of a lamb or beef joint
- 2 carrots
- 2 onions cut into quarters
- Celery
- Parsnip (optional)
- Seasoning (bay leaf, parsley, thyme, salt, pepper corns)
- Water to cover

Method

1. Put all the ingredients in the pan and bring the stock to the boil
2. Skim off any scum on the surface
3. Cover and simmer for 2-3 hours
4. Sieve the stock and leave to cool
5. Leave in a cool place until the fat has formed a hard layer on the top
6. Spoon the fat off the top and store stock in the fridge, or freeze in a plastic container

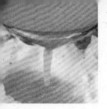

Basic **STOCK – POULTRY**

 10 60+

Suitable for

Leftover poultry carcass, scraps of poultry and leftover vegetables.

Ingredients

- 1 chicken or turkey carcass (preferably with giblets if you have them) and any leftover chicken or turkey meat
- 2 rashers bacon (optional)
- 2 onions cut into quarters
- 2 carrots cut into quarters
- 1 chicken stock cube (optional)
- Water (enough to cover the carcass in the saucepan)
- Salt
- 8 peppercorns
- Bouquet garni or a pinch of thyme, rosemary, tarragon and parsley

Method

1. Chop up the onion and bacon (if using) and fry in a large saucepan for 2 minutes.
2. Add the carcass and all the other ingredients
3. Bring the stock to the boil over a high heat. Then reduce the heat and let the stock simmer gently for 2-3 hours
4. When the stock has cooled a little, strain it through a sieve
5. Leave in a cool place until the fat has formed a hard layer on the top
6. Spoon the fat off the top and store stock in the fridge, or freeze in a plastic container

Basic **STOCK – VEGETABLE**

🕐 10 🕐 55

Suitable for

'Lone' raw vegetables.

Ingredients

- 1 onion, cut in quarters
- 4-5 of either/combination of carrots, parsnips, swede or mushrooms
- 1 leek
- Chopped celery (optional}
- Fresh parsley or a pinch of dry parsley
- Salt and pepper
- 3-4 pints water

Method

① Put all ingredients in a large saucepan, bring to the boil and simmer for 1½ hours
② Sieve and allow to cool
③ Store in the fridge or freeze

Individual **recipes**

APPLE AND CINNAMON FRITTERS 🕐 15 🕐 10

Suitable for

Slightly crinkly apples (or bananas).

Ingredients

- 3 tablespoons vegetable oil
- 2 apples
- 110g plain flour
- Pinch of caster sugar
- Salt
- 1 egg
- ¼ pint/150ml milk

To serve

Sprinkle of caster sugar (optional) • sprinkle of cinnamon (optional) • double cream to drizzle (or natural yoghurt) • honey to drizzle (optional).

Method

1. Heat the oil in a saucepan
2. Peel the apples and core them using a corer or sharp knife
3. Slice the apples into rings, or bananas lengthways
4. Place the flour, sugar and salt into a large bowl. Gradually beat in the egg and enough milk (about ¼ pint/150 ml) to form a batter
5. Dip the apple rings into the batter to coat well and fry until golden (about 3-4 minutes).
6. Remove the fritters from the oil with a slotted spoon and drain on absorbent kitchen paper
7. Sprinkle generously with sugar and cinnamon
8. Serve drizzled with cream and honey

BAKED CHEESY POTATOES

 10  5

Suitable for

Cooked baked potato, old or hard cheese.

Ingredients

- 1 cooked baked potato
- 1 teaspoon of crème fraîche
- 25g grated cheddar cheese
- 1 teaspoon Worcestershire sauce
- Pinch of cayenne pepper (optional)

Method

❶ Cut the potato in half

❷ Remove the inside of the potato with a spoon

❸ Mix the potato with crème fraîche, grated cheddar cheese, Worcestershire sauce and cayenne pepper

❹ When the ingredients are really well mixed, spoon the mixture back into the potato skins

❹ Grill for 5 minutes

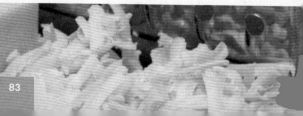

BAKED POTATO FILLINGS

 10 10 60

Suitable for

Cooked chicken, leftover stew, curry or tomato sauce, old or hard cheese, cooked roast vegetables – the possibilities are endless.

Chicken mayonnaise with sweet corn (C)

❶ Mix 50g of cooked chicken with 1 tablespoon mayonnaise and ½ small tin of sweet corn

❷ Add black pepper to taste and a sprinkling of grated cheese on top

Curried chicken (C)

❶ Mix 50g of cooked chicken with 1 tablespoon mayonnaise and a pinch of curry powder

❷ Add a small handful of raisins or sliced up grapes

Tuna and tomato sauce (S)

❶ Use up any tomato pasta sauce by adding ½ tin of tuna and mixing well

❷ Heat well and serve

Crème fraîche/natural yoghurt with red onion and red pepper (L)

❶ Mix the last scrapings of a pot of crème fraîche or natural yoghurt into the mixture
❷ Fry half a chopped red onion and half a red pepper until soft

Curry/stew/bolognaise (C)

❶ Heat up the leftover curry, bolognaise or stew in a saucepan
❷ If the leftovers are a little dry, add a spoonful of crème fraîche, cream or natural yoghurt and stir in well

Roast vegetables (C)

- Re-heat the roasted vegetables in a saucepan, stirring all the time
- Serve with lots of black pepper and grated parmesan cheese (optional)

Other fillings

- *Baked beans*
- *Chopped bacon*
- *Chopped ham*
- *Grated cheese*

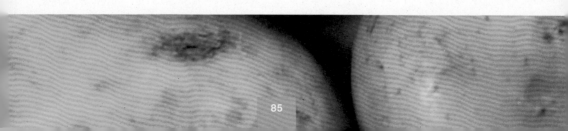

BANANA AND CHOCOLATE DIGESTIVE PUDDING

 10 + 60 in fridge

Suitable for

Over-ripe bananas and old biscuits.

Ingredients

- 3 or 4 ripe bananas (depending on the size)
- 250g natural yoghurt (or double cream)
- 2 tablespoons brown sugar
- 6 or 7 chocolate digestive biscuits (or any other leftover biscuits or crumbs in the bottom of the biscuit tin)
- squeeze of lemon juice (optional)

Method

1. Mash up the bananas in a flat-bottomed dish
2. Add the yoghurt, brown sugar and lemon juice and mix well
3. Tear off two sheets of kitchen roll (still attached to each other) and lay out flat
4. Roughly break the biscuits onto one sheet of the kitchen roll and fold the second sheet over the top of the biscuits
5. Crush the biscuits inside the kitchen roll, make sure you crush all the lumps
6. Sprinkle crushed biscuits on top of the banana mix and flatten down with a fork
7. Put the pudding in the fridge for an hour

BEAN AND ONION STEW

Suitable for

Leftover onions and canned beans.

🕐 5   🕐 10

Ingredients

- 2 tablespoons vegetable or olive oil
- 1 large onion, chopped
- 1 teaspoon of cumin
- 1 teaspoon of ground coriander
- 1 x 400g can chickpeas (or canellini or haricot beans)
- 1 x 400g can chopped tomatoes
- Sprig fresh coriander (optional)
- Bread rolls

Method

1. Heat the oil over a medium heat and then add the onions
2. Cook for about 3 minutes until golden and soft
3. Add the cumin and stir it into the onions
4. Add the tin of chickpeas, or other beans, and the tin of tomatoes
5. Simmer gently until all the ingredients are absorbed
6. Serve with a sprig of coriander on the top and a some fresh bread

BREAD AND BUTTER PUDDING

🕐 10 🕐 35

Suitable for

Old bread.

Ingredients

- 8 slices buttered bread cut in half diagonally
- Rind of lemon or orange (grated)
- 40g sultanas or currants
- 250 ml full fat milk
- 70 ml double cream
- 50g caster sugar
- 3 eggs
- Nutmeg
- Lemon/orange rind (optional)
- Chocolate chips (optional)

Method

1. Pre-heat the oven to 180°C/350°F/Gas mark 4
2. Place one layer of the bread into the base of a well buttered baking dish and sprinkle over some sultanas
3. Repeat with another layer of bread and sultanas and carry on with the layers until all the bread and sultanas are used
4. Beat the egg, milk, cream, peel and sugar together and then pour over the bread
5. Grate some nutmeg over the top and bake in the oven for 35 minutes. The top should be golden and crisp-looking when it's finished

BUBBLE AND SQUEAK

 5 10

Suitable for

Cooked mashed potato; cooked greens, cabbage, Brussels sprouts.

Ingredients

- 4 portions of mashed potato
- 400g (ish) of cooked cabbage/greens/Brussels sprouts
- 4 rashers of chopped streaky bacon (optional)
- 2 tablespoons sweet corn (optional)
- 50 g vegetable oil

Method

❶ Fry bacon in non-stick frying pan until nicely browned
❷ Meanwhile mash together the veggies and potato, season with salt and pepper
❸ Add them to the bacon and fry the mixture in the oil for about 4 minutes on each side, until it is crispy and golden brown

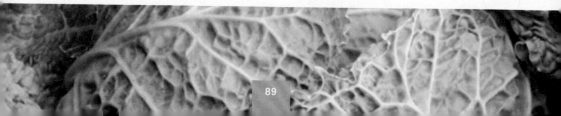

CHICKEN CRUNCH

⏱ 15   ⏱ 20

Suitable for

Cooked chicken or turkey; cooked or 'lonely' vegetables; or hard cheese;
old bread (breadcrumbs)

Ingredients

- 500g chicken or turkey meat and 200g broccoli or leeks
- 1 small tin sweet corn, 50g butter plus 2 tablespoons plain flour
- 250ml milk/vegetable water
- 1 dessert spoon mayonnaise and 1 dessert spoon lemon/lime juice
- 200g grated cheese and salt & pepper
- 1 packet of crisps/3 tablespoons old bread

Method

1. Pre-heat the oven at 200°C/400°F/gas mark 6
2. Cut the broccoli into small florets and cook for 10 minutes, keeping the water from the pan to use later in the sauce if you wish
3. Put the chicken and broccoli into a flat-bottomed oven-proof dish and add the drained sweet corn
4. Melt the butter in a saucepan and blend in the flour
5. Gradually blend in the milk, stirring constantly over a medium heat until the sauce becomes thick and smooth. Use broccoli water instead of some/all of the milk if you wish
6. When you have a reasonably thick sauce, add the mayonnaise, lemon/lime juice and half the grated cheese and stir in well. Add salt and pepper to taste
7. Pour the sauce over the chicken, broccoli and sweet corn. Crunch the crisps until there are no big bits of crisp left and sprinkle the contents evenly over the chicken and sauce, followed by the remains of the grated cheese
8. If you don't have crisps then breadcrumbs can be used
9. Bake in the oven for about 15 to 20 minutes until golden

CHILLI CON CARNE

⏱ 10 ⏱ 50

Suitable for

Cooked minced or diced beef.

Ingredients

If you do not have enough cooked beef leftover, bulk out the recipe with either more tinned kidney beans or a tin of flageolet, cannellini or haricot beans.

- 400-500g cooked beef, either minced or in chunks
- 1 large onion, chopped and 1 clove of garlic, crushed
- 1 x 400g tin of kidney beans, drained
- ½ a teaspoon chilli powder or 1 fresh chilli, de-seeded and chopped
- 1-2 peppers, de-seeded and chopped
- 1 (400g) tin chopped tomatoes and 2 bay leaves
- 200ml stock or water
- 1 tablespoon sunflower oil, salt and pepper

Method

① Heat the oil in a deep frying pan, add the onions and cook for 3-4 minutes until golden
② Add the garlic, peppers and fresh chillies or chilli powder and cook for another 2 minutes
③ Add the tinned tomatoes and the kidney beans (and any other beans you may be using as a meat substitute) and cover the contents with stock
④ Add the bay leaves and simmer for 30 minutes
⑤ After 30 minutes add the minced meat and continue to simmer for another 10 minutes.
⑥ Serve with baked potatoes or rice with a dollop of sour cream if available and a green salad on the side

CHOCOLATE CRISPY CAKES

 10

Suitable for

Any kind of crisp cereal, e.g. rice crispies or cornflakes.

Ingredients

- 225g plain chocolate
- 3 tablespoons golden syrup (or maple syrup)
- 50g margarine
- 100g crisp cereal (e.g. cornflakes)

Method

1. Grease the inside of a 20cm diameter round shallow tin using a little butter. (Keep old butter wrappers in the fridge as the remaining film of butter on them is perfect for greasing baking tins.) Try not to leave too much butter on the tin
2. Break the chocolate into a large pan. Add the syrup and margarine
3. Heat the pan gently, stirring all the time
4. When the chocolate has melted, add the cornflakes or rice crispies and stir well so that they are coated all over in the chocolate
5. Spoon the mixture into the tin. Gently smooth the top with the back of a spoon. Let the mixture cool
6. Put tin in the fridge until chocolate has set – roughly two hours.
7. Use a sharp knife to cut it into eight pieces

FISH CAKES

⏱ 10 ⏱ 5

Suitable for

Cooked filleted fish; canned fish; cooked mashed potato; old bread.

Ingredients

- 2 tins sardines/tuna or 275g of cooked fillet of any fish
- 4 portions of mashed potato
- 2 tomatoes (optional)
- 2 spring onion (finely sliced)
- leftover peas (2 portions maximum)
- 1 egg
- 10 tablespoons breadcrumbs made with old bread
- 3 tablespoons oil
- 25g butter
- Lemon wedges for serving

Method

1. Mash the fish, potatoes, tomato, spring onions, peas and egg together with a fork
2. Season with salt and pepper
3. Divide mixture into 8 and shape into patties
4. Roll in breadcrumbs
5. Heat up oil and butter in large frying pan (preferably non-stick) and, when hot, add fish cakes
6. Fry for about 2 minutes on each side taking care not to let the butter burn
7. Serve immediately. Delicious served with a green salad and sweet chilli sauce

FRUIT JUICES

 5

For all the recipes below, put all the ingredients into a blender and blend until smooth. If you want to remove any pips, pass the juice through a sieve before serving.

Suitable for

All leftover or over-ripe fruit.

Fruit punch

- 6 strawberries/raspberries, fresh or thawed from frozen
- 1 apple, cored, peeled and sliced
- ½ orange, peeled and segmented (or 50ml orange juice)
- 100ml water

Peach, pear and apple juice

- 1 apple, cored, peeled and sliced
- 2 peaches, peeled and stoned
- 1 pear peeled, cored and sliced

Cranberry crush

- 1 red grapefruit, peeled and segmented
- 2 medium oranges, peeled and segmented
- 3 handfuls cranberries (or 200ml cranberry juice)

Lemon and lime ginger ale

- 2 handfuls of grapes
- 1 apple, cored, peeled and sliced
- 1cm fresh ginger, peeled and chopped
- Juice of one lime
- Juice of half a lemon
- Sparkling water

  Mix all the fruit and juice in a blender. Pour into a glass and top up with the sparkling water and ice

Strawberry/raspberry zing

- 2 handfuls of strawberries/raspberries
- 2 medium apples, peeled, cored and sliced
- Juice of ½ lemon

Other fruits that are delicious 'juiced up':

- *Blueberries*
- *Blackcurrants*
- *Cherries*
- *Grapes*
- *Melon*
- *Peaches*

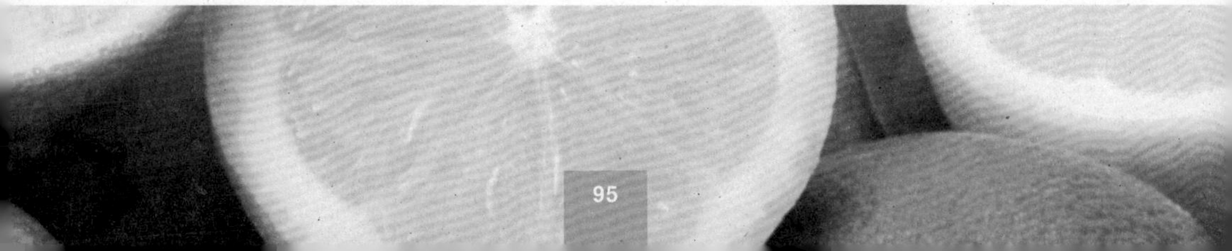

ICED COFFEE

Suitable for

Leftover coffee.

⏱ 5

Ingredients

- 1 cup of cold black coffee
- Milk to taste
- Sugar to taste
- Ice cubes
- 1 drop vanilla essence (optional)

Method

1. Pour some of the coffee into an ice cube tray and freeze
2. Warm the coffee over a low heat for a couple of minutes – or microwave for about 1 minute
3. Add the sugar if wanted
4. Let the coffee go cold and add the vanilla essence and milk if using. Stir well
5. Fill a tall glass with ice/your coffee ice cubes, and pour the coffee over the top
6. Whipped cream on top of iced coffee jazzes it up a bit

LAMB PITTA POCKETS

⏱ 10 ⏱ 5

Suitable for

Cooked lamb, beef or chicken.

Ingredients

- A small knob of butter
- 1 chopped red/white onion
- 1 sliced red pepper
- 300g diced cooked lamb
- 4 pitta bread
- sour cream to taste

Method

❶ Heat the pitta bread in a toaster

❷ Melt the knob of butter in a frying pan and add the chopped onion and slices of raw red pepper. Cook until the onion is translucent and the pepper soft

❸ Slice the pitta bread open along the side from one end to the other and spread the inside of the pitta with sour cream

❹ Fill the pitta pocket with the diced lamb and spoon in some of the onion and peppers

❺ Serve with a green salad

LEMON VINAIGRETTE

 10

Suitable for

Old lemons.

Ingredients

- 5 tablespoons extra-virgin olive oil (can use hazelnut or walnut oil)
- 2 tablespoons freshly squeezed lemon juice
- ½ teaspoon Dijon-style mustard
- 3/4 teaspoon fresh thyme leaves, chopped
- 1 clove garlic, crushed
- 3/4 teaspoon coarse salt
- Pinch freshly cracked black pepper

Method

❶ Combine all the ingredients together and stir really well

❷ Store in a bottle with a good sealing lid or cork so that the vinaigrette can be vigorously shaken before each use

MACARONI CHEESE

 5   10

This is a basic recipe, to which you can add cooked ham, bacon, sausage, chicken, tomatoes or sweetcorn if you wish.

Suitable for

Cooked pasta; old or hard cheese.

Ingredients

- 100g cooked pasta per person
- 50g butter
- 2 tablespoons flour
- 250ml milk
- 70g grated cheddar cheese
- 1 teaspoon grainy mustard (optional) plus salt and pepper
- Grated cheese or breadcrumbs for topping

Method

❶ Put the pasta into a medium-sized, flat-bottomed oven-proof dish.

❷ Melt the butter in a saucepan and blend in the flour.

❸ Gradually blend in the milk, stirring constantly over a medium heat until the sauce becomes thick and smooth

❹ Add the cheese and mustard and any other leftover ingredients. Mix the sauce well and pour over the pasta

❺ Top with further grated cheese or breadcrumbs and place under a hot grill for about 5 minutes or until the topping goes crispy and starts to brown. Delicious also with sliced tomatoes, grated cheese or breadcrumbs on top

QUICK TOMATO AND LENTIL SOUP ⏱ 5 ⏱ 15

This is both a 'leftover' recipe – it is a great way to use up rather soft tomatoes – and one that can be rustled up in a hurry using the basics in the cupboard.

Suitable for

Lentils (from the store cupboard); slightly soft tomatoes.

Ingredients

- 1 medium-sized onion chopped
- 1 clove garlic
- 4 medium-sized tomatoes chopped or 1 x 400g tin of chopped tomatoes
- 1 stock cube (vegetable or chicken)
- 2 handfuls of red lentils
- 1 teaspoon pesto (optional)
- pinch of mixed herbs
- salt and pepper to taste

Method

1. Make the stock cube up in a litre of stock
2. Pour stock and tinned tomato into a medium-sized saucepan. Extra flavour can be had by adding the dregs of a pot of yeast extract (e.g. Marmite).
3. Add the lentils to the pan and heat over a medium heat until the soup is simmering
4. Add the pesto, mixed herbs and salt and pepper to taste
5. Simmer for about 15 minutes or until the lentils are soft

SAUSAGE SPECIAL FRIED RICE

This is also delicious using diced cooked pork.

⏱ 5 ⏱ 15

Suitable for

Cooked sausages or pork; cooked rice

Ingredients

- 25g butter
- 2 eggs – beaten
- 1 onion (chopped)
- 4 helpings cooked rice
- 3-4 leftover cooked sausages – sliced or 200g diced cooked pork
- 2 handfuls frozen peas (or leftover cooked peas)
- 2 handfuls frozen or tinned sweet corn
- 3 spring onions, chopped (optional)
- Soy sauce to taste

Method

1. Melt the butter in a frying pan over a medium heat and then add onion. Cook for about 3 minutes
2. Add the beaten egg and cook for 1 minute, stirring constantly
3. Using a fork, break up the cooked egg and stir in the cooked rice, sliced up sausage, peas and sweet corn and desired amount of soy sauce
4. Heat gently, stirring constantly, for about 5-7 minutes

SCONES

🕐 10 🕐 10

Suitable for

Slightly sour milk.

Ingredients

- 225g self-raising flour
- ½ teaspoon baking powder
- Pinch of salt
- 50g butter or margarine
- 25g caster sugar
- 150ml milk (slightly 'off' milk can be used)
- 50g sultanas (optional)
- Extra milk for glazing
  (Makes about 16 scones)

Method

1. Pre-heat the oven to 230°C/450°F/gas mark 8. Grease two baking sheets with butter or margarine
2. Sift flour, baking powder and salt into a bowl. Cut up the butter or margarine into the flour and rub it into the flour using your fingertips.
3. Add the sugar, milk and sultanas, mix to a soft dough and mould it into a ball
4. Roll out the dough on a floured worktop until it is about 1 cm thick
5. Using a 6cm diameter round cutter cut the dough into circles. Squeeze the scraps into a ball and repeat until all the dough has been used
6. Put the circles on the baking sheets, leaving about 5cm between each one
7. Brush the tops with milk and bake in the oven for 7-10 minutes until the scones have risen and turned golden
8. Lift them onto a wire rack to cool
9. Serve with butter or clotted cream (optional) and strawberry jam

SPANISH OMELETTE

 5 15

Suitable for

Cooked potatoes; cooked or leftover ham or bacon; cooked vegetables (peas, leeks, courgettes, French beans); old or hard cheese.

Ingredients

- 1 tablespoon vegetable oil
- 1 red or white onion
- Streaky bacon/leftover ham/chorizo – chopped (optional)
- 3 cooked potatoes
- 100g cooked vegetables (peas, French beans, leeks)
- 3-4 eggs
- 3 tablespoons of milk
- 50g grated Cheddar cheese
- Salt and pepper to taste

Method

❶ Break the eggs into a bowl, add milk, salt and pepper and beat with a fork until blended

❷ Heat the vegetable oil in a deep, non-stick frying pan over a medium heat. Add onions and fry gently until they are translucent and slightly brown. Add the bacon or ham or chorizo and cook for about 3 minutes

❸ Chop the cooked potatoes into chunks and add these to the frying pan stirring all the time. Add any leftover vegetables and heat through

❹ Add the egg mixture to the pan and add the grated cheese on top

❺ Lower the heat and cover the pan with a lid. Cook the omelette for about 12 minutes until the egg has hardened

❻ Remove from the heat, cut the omelette into wedges and serve immediately

STUFFED PEPPERS WITH RICE

 10 ⏱ 35

Suitable for

Cooked, chopped bacon, cooked and sliced mushrooms, cooked broccoli, leeks, spinach or peas, diced ham, cooked chopped onion, cheese.

Ingredients

- 8 peppers (yellow, red or green)
- 2 onions (finely chopped)
- 1 tablespoon of oil
- 2 large clove garlic
- 1 x 400g tin chopped tomatoes or 6 large tomatoes, chopped
- Any leftover ingredients as above: bacon, ham or vegetables
- 400g cooked rice (any kind will do)
- 4 sprigs of fresh parsley/3 teaspoons dried parsley
- 2 teaspoons dried oregano, salt and pepper to taste

Method

1. Pre-heat the oven to 190°C/375°F/gas mark 5
2. Cut the tops off the peppers (around the stalk) and spoon or cut out all the white bits and seeds inside. Keep the 'lids' of the peppers
3. Drain the juice from the tomatoes. If using fresh tomatoes, separate the flesh of the tomato from the juice as much as possible
4. Fry the chopped onion in the oil over a medium heat for 2 minutes. Add the garlic and fry for a further minute
5. In a bowl, mix the tomatoes, cooked rice, oregano, parsley, onions and garlic plus the bacon, ham or vegetables, if using these. Season well
6. Put the peppers, open end up, on a deep baking tray. Spoon the rice mixture into the peppers so that they have equal amounts in each. Replace the lids on the peppers
7. Fill the baking tray with a little water (about half an inch) – this will prevent the peppers from burning – and put them in the oven for 30 minutes until peppers are cooked
8. Serve warm with a green salad

SUMMER PUDDING

🕐 20 + overnight to chill/soak

Suitable for

Slightly soft or leftover cooked summer fruit, e.g.: strawberries, blackcurrants, redcurrants, blueberries, raspberries, blackberries; old bread. You will need a round 1 litre pudding bowl.

Ingredients

- 750g mixed summer fruit: e.g. blackcurrants, redcurrants, blackberries, blueberries
- 180g caster sugar
- 7-8 slices of white bread from a large loaf
- 2 tablespoons water(if not enough juice)

Method

❶ Stew the fruit by placing it all in a big saucepan (having removed all the stems) with the water and the sugar. Cook gently over a medium heat for about 3-5 minutes. Leave to cool

❷ Line the bowl with the slices of bread, making sure you overlap them and press down hard to seal any gaps

❸ Pour the fruit and the juice (keeping back half a cup of juice) into the bread-lined bowl

❹ Cover the top with another slice or two of bread

❺ Find a plate that fits neatly into the top of the bowl and place it on the top. Put something heavy on the plate to weigh it down.

❻ Place the bowl in the fridge, on a large plate (to catch any stray juice) Leave over night so that the bread soaks up the juices

❼ Before serving, turn out the pudding onto a large plate, spoon over the extra fruit juice

❽ Serve with cream or natural yoghurt

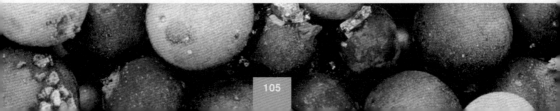

VEGETABLE STEW

 15   20-40

Vegetable stew is the best way to use up any lonely, maybe slightly wrinkly vegetables. Just about any combination of vegetables will do.

Suitable for

Winter stew: leftover parsnips, swede, turnip, potato, carrot, sweet potato, butternut squash, celery, lentils

Summer stew: leftover French beans , broad beans, courgette, carrots, mushrooms, tomatoes, red peppers

Ingredients

- 900g combination of vegetables (as above)
- 3 tablespoons oil
- 2 onions, 2 cloves garlic
- 1 x 400g tinned tomatoes
- 500ml vegetable stock
- 1 tablespoon tomato purée
- 2 celery sticks, salt and pepper
  Optional Ingredients: 1 teaspoon ground cumin • 1 teaspoon ground coriander
  • 1 teaspoon chilli powder • 1-2 teaspoon Worcestershire sauce

Method

1. Wash, peel, core and chop all the vegetables to bite-sized chunks
2. Heat the oil and cook the onions for 2 minutes. Add the garlic, and any spices or chilli (if using), and cook for a further minute
3. Add the remaining vegetables and cook for about 3 minutes, stirring all the time.
4. Add the stock, tomato purée and Worcestershire sauce, if using, and season with salt and pepper
5. Bring to the boil, then reduce the heat. For summer vegetables, simmer for about 15 minutes, for winter vegetables, 35-40 minutes until the vegetables are cooked.

WELSH RAREBIT

🕐 5   🕐 5

Suitable for

Leftover cooked ham, old or hard cheese.

Ingredients

- 200g grated, strong cheese such as Cheddar or Cheshire
- 1 tablespoon butter
- 2 teaspoons Worcestershire sauce
- 1 level teaspoon dry mustard
- 2 teaspoons flour
- 4 tablespoons milk
- 4 slices ham, chopped
- Pepper to taste
- 4 slices bread toasted on 1 side only

Method

1. Mix the cheese, flour, mustard, Worcestershire sauce, butter and pepper in a bowl and transfer to a small, non-stick saucepan
2. Add the milk and stir over a gentle heat until all the ingredients has melted so that it forms a thickish sauce. Add the chopped ham as required
3. Leave to cool slightly
4. Meanwhile lightly toast the bread
5. Spread the sauce over the untoasted side of the bread and brown under a hot grill

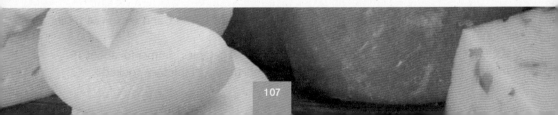

Also available from Green Books:

Composting:
an easy household guide
by Nicky Scott

Tells you everything you need to know
for successful home composting.

£4.95 paperback

Reduce, Reuse, Recycle
by Nicky Scott

Includes an A–Z guide for household recycling.

£4.95 paperback

For our complete list of books, see www.greenbooks.co.uk